Convent Life and Beyond

Grace E. Stoltz

Outskirts Press, Inc.
Denver, Colorado

Outskirts Press
http://www.outskirtspress.com

ISBN-13: 978-1-4327-0594-7

Outskirts Press and the "OP" logo are trademarks belonging to
Outskirts Press, Inc.

Printed in the United States of America

Dedication and Acknowledgments

This narrative is dedicated to all the students from North Dakota, Illinois, Georgia, Venezuela and Minnesota who were at any time under my influence. Each one of them holds a special place in my heart even though their names and faces may slowly fade from my memory as the years begin to take their exacting toll in this my seventy-seventh year.

Also included in this dedication are the many devoted servants of the Lord in my life: nuns, priests, bible study friends, neighbors, friends and family who have given me a better image of the way God is constantly drawing us to his love. These people have shown me the love of God, have helped me mature in my Christian walk and are a constant reminder that all things work for good when we place our trust in his way, his truth, and his life.

Some of these people who have crossed my path have encouraged me to write of my experiences in the convent.

Some are just curious about why I joined a convent and why I eventually left it. Former students want to know what was going on in my personal life during the time I was their teacher. Others want me to tell of the many experiences of teaching that have provided much joy, humor, and consolation in my life.

To all who may read these pages, know that my purpose is not to hide the truth nor place the blame for any of my mistakes on anyone else's shoulders. My botches, bungles, and blunders are my own. Along the way, I have disagreed with other Christians about how to apply the message of Jesus to my life. I was not always right. They were not always wrong. I believe we can learn from our experiences and move on to stand shoulder to shoulder with each other as we discern how to lighten each other's burdens and help bring heaven down here into our lives that can be hellish without the love of God to give our lives meaning.

Most personal names used in this story are fictitious as are the names of many of the towns mentioned. However, the stories are factual as far as my memory recalls them.

I wish to thank my cousin Jim Noonan and my friends Julie Boyle, Peggy Cremers, Sharlene Scheller and Mary Kaye Wright who offered suggestions to make this narrative more readable.

If you are interested in more details about life as lived in small town North Dakota prior to my convent life, you may refer to my first book entitled, *Narratives of Grace*. You may obtain copies at Barnes & Noble or Amazon online bookstores.

Preface

This book contains my personal opinions concerning how God worked in mysterious ways in my life and how he constantly guides all to appreciate his love and plans for our good.

As pilgrim believers in the message of Jesus Christ, we all make the journey through life, trying to be a light to those around us, extending a helping hand, doing our part to show that God is with us every step of the way.

We may start out on this journey, fresh and eager -- honored that we are called to partner with God in his desire to draw all people to himself in love and peace. Then we may stumble, become confused, stray from his way, repent, and continue as the Holy Spirit transforms our minds and hearts. Relentlessly, the Holy Spirit keeps at his work of renovating us from the inside out. He begins to change our attitudes and give us a fresh way of thinking. He takes his time, letting us reach out for help and clarification, as we grow stronger and more trusting.

Life is never static—especially life in Christ. As his

followers, we need to be prepared to orient ourselves anew each day, to be ready to seek a new path if God calls us to it. We know we are on the right path when his gospel is our criterion. With the banner of his Word to assure us of his constant presence in our every circumstance, we can boldly go forward in his name. When one path is closed off to us, we have the comfort of knowing he will faithfully point out another and accompany us on our way. With those biblical principles implanted deep in our hearts, we can proceed with confidence because of the promises Jesus gives us in the following two passages:

"Ask and you will receive; seek and you will find; knock and the door will be opened to you."
Luke 11:9

"Therefore, since we have a great high priest who has passed through the heavens, Jesus, the Son of God, let us hold fast to our confession. For we do not have a high priest who is unable to sympathize with our weaknesses, but one who has similarly been tested in every way, yet without sin. So let us confidently approach the throne of grace to receive mercy and to find grace for timely help."
Hebrews 4:14-16

Book One
A Rookie in Training

Test everything; retain what is good.
1 Thessalonians 5:21

Fools rush in where angels fear to tread.
Essay on Criticism, Part III, Line 66
Alexander Pope

Introduction

Frenzied Night Fears of a Panicky Postulant

It hurts so much! What is building this wall around me, crushing me in from all sides? What am I doing here? Why am I lying here cringing in fear? What has taken away my sense of fun? Where has my joy and happiness gone? This can't be happening to me! This is not what I expected! My stomach is in knots, burning from anxiety. I thirst for holiness but this can't be the way to get it. This just doesn't make sense! What am I doing in this convent where all the prayers are in French? I don't even know when to say the French Amen ("Ainsi soit-il") when the community finally finishes those long-drawn-out, never-changing prayers recited before the sun is up.

Can I survive this kind of life? No, I was wrong not to listen to my mother and to Mother Marie, my counselor at boarding school. They knew me better than I knew myself. Why am I always so impulsive? Will I ever learn?

If I had just listened to Mother Marie, I could be right

1

back there in the boarding school now, doing all the things girls my age are supposed to do. Those days were so much fun. I was learning so much and enjoying every minute of it after I got used to being away from home. Yes, those first days at boarding school were scary but nothing like this. In that place, it didn't take me long to adjust, find friends and so much satisfaction from learning about Jesus from the wonderful nuns who taught me new things everyday.

I wonder if Dolly and all the rest of my boarder friends miss me at all. For sure, I know that they will never get a letter or message through to me. That would be like trying to break down a locked door with a toothpick. I am in jail, but I chose to slam this door on myself without having the slightest guarantee that this choice is what God wants for me.

All right now! Snap out of it! I am going to remember what my wise sister Aggie told me when I had just made a whopper mistake. "Don't live by guilt and what if's. Leave your mistakes behind and go on."

Aggie gave me that advice right after her son, Jim, had been lost for hours because I had failed to watch over him as I had promised.

Okay! Chin up! I will take whatever comes my way. Maybe I will get used to this life originating from one woman's strange ideas of what it takes to become holy. Mother Gertrude seems to be trying to squeeze me into some kind of alien mold that is just not meant for me. She expects me to walk, talk, work and pray like a prim and proper nun from the start. I can't change my habits that fast!

Ha! Ha! That is kind of funny! She thinks I can change my ways as easily as she puts on her "habit" every morning when she dresses. Sober up! This is no time to be joking! I won't give up on my first days in this convent. I asked for it. Now it is time to just get on with it.

Oh, dear, if I don't get some sleep tonight, I will never

be able to get up when that clanging bell wakes me in the morning. *I pray when Mother Gertrude calls out, "Blessed be God forever," I will be able to answer wholeheartedly with the required response, "Let us rise to do God's will." I will honestly try.*

Chapter 1
Challenges and Changes

My impetuous nature, my naive ideas, and my deep yearning to serve the Lord led me to St. Caitlin's Convent in Valley Center, North Dakota where I would spend months learning what is expected of girls who aspire to be nuns. This happened in February of 1945 just after I turned 15 years of age.

Mother Marie, the head nun at my boarding school had sent me home to confer with my mother about *my* idea of entering the convent. My sailor brother, Gene, was home on leave. He had left for the Navy when he was only seventeen. He tried to convince me to listen to reason and stay in school. He argued, "Grace, you just don't know what you are getting yourself into. Are you trying to escape something unpleasant at school? Are your teachers picking on you?"

Indignantly I replied, "Absolutely not! I love boarding

school life. The teachers are great and that is what I want to be, a teaching nun. I want to get started on that dream right now."

Relentlessly, he continued, "You will be a better teacher if you continue your education in a normal setting. Maybe you should even come back home to finish here in our good Verona public school."

"No way! You are a fine one to advise me. You didn't finish high school before you went off to serve your country. I want to serve God. That's even better!"

"I am not so sure about that. Anyway, my case is different. Our country is at war! And I fully intend to come back home when the war is over to finish my schooling. My time in the Navy so far has taught me education is important if a person wants to make a go of it in this world."

We spent a couple of days arguing but when he had to leave, we were still on the best of terms. Gene and I were always close. I was in tears and he was very close to them as he waved goodbye boarding the bus to get back to his patriotic duties.

After he left, my mother took up the arguments against my desire to enter the convent. When she got tired my sister, Mary, took over the task. She was living in the state of Washington where her Army husband, Harold, was stationed. Mom made a call to her to ask for her help. Mary knew something about the life of nuns because she had been a church secretary on a North Dakota Indian reservation where several nuns were teachers. I had to laugh at one of her desperate arguments: "Grace, do you know that the main meals of the nuns consist of liver and prunes?"

She knew that I hate both of those foods. But after we finished laughing about that ridiculous ploy, Mary quickly got very serious. She couldn't talk long because phone calls were expensive. Her opinions as well as Mom's focused on my lack of experience in making life-changing decisions, on my tendency to leap into things without mature evaluation, and on what I would miss of the normal and necessary parts of growing up like dating, chumming around with friends, and holding down a job.

Despite all the protests from my mother and my siblings, I was adamant about becoming a nun. I told them how much my teachers had helped me come to know Jesus better and that is what I wanted to do for others.

Reluctantly, my mother gave her consent. Her mind, at the time, was distracted with concerns for three of my older brothers who had enlisted in various branches of the military service. Gene joined the Navy in 1942. Don was far off in Germany serving as a medic and Ralph (We all called him Sam) was somewhere in Africa, both Army recruits. Harold, the brother just two years older than me, told me that his training as a Marine would begin as soon as he finished high school in May. Ultimately, I suppose my mother felt comforted by the thought that at least I would be safe in the convent until I came to my senses. She was quite sure I would not last long.

So, at age fifteen, my childhood ended abruptly the day I traveled by bus to the convent on Valentine's Day, 1945. After halfway remembering the reasons others had given me about the folly of forgoing normal adolescent experiences, this trip gave me a chance to look back at the happy years I had spent with friends and family in my hometown of Verona. As the bus rolled on toward my future at the convent in Valley Center, many pleasant recollections of family filled this travel time along with the cherished memories of my hometown life.

Harold and Gene's "Purple Pocket" adventures popped into my mind. Those two had fashioned a small but deep hole in the backyard complete with a sod-covered hinged door. With their vivid imaginations, they used this hideout to plan their many mischievous pranks. They had held Millie and me captive in their infamous dungeon a few times until Mom put a stop to that. Because of all their naughtiness, they acquired the nicknames of two comic strip characters, Hans and Fritz, known as "The Katzenjammer Kids." Fritz became the permanent name for Harold but Hans never did stick to Gene for long. No matter what they did, Millie and I idolized these two brothers who were next to us in age: At this time, Gene was 19 and Fritz was 17, and Mildred was 13.

When we first moved to town from our farm in 1934, the four of us youngest in our family of ten spent many happy hours together in the summer, playing softball, visiting the stockyards, watching the daily passenger and freight trains steam up the track to the depot. After the passengers had disembarked and the train whistled on its merry way, we balanced our steps on the railroad tracks, climbed the boxcars to get a better view of our town, played tag, Run Sheep Run, and Kick the Can with all the other children in town.

For entertainment during the winter months, we played Monopoly indoors, listened to the radio or we made ice cream using the abundant snow to cool the ingredients as we took turns churning the crank on the cumbersome ice-cream maker. Outdoors, with our friends, we designed immense many-roomed snow houses in the packed drifts along the fences located near the railroad tracks.

Lil, the sister just two years older than Gene, also added moments of entertainment to our childhood days. Gene, Fritz, Mildred and I adored this lovely red-haired sister, Yet, we also enjoyed teasing her about her many boyfriends, her attempts to sneak up to her room to smoke a cigarette and her tendency to pout whenever she didn't get her way.

Agnes, our oldest sister, had invited Millie and me to spend a few days with her in LaMoure on several occasions. She had opened her own beauty shop in her apartment. She was always so sweet-tempered even after her long hours of work. During the day, we played outdoors in the park just across the street or we watched in fascination as she gave perms or hair cuts to her many customers.

The perm process made us decide we would rather have straight hair than risk having our tresses curled up in rollers attached to a nest of wires dangling from that frightful looking perm contraption.

As the miles continued to roll by, I also wondered if my childhood sweetheart, Richard Taylor, would miss me. We had been pals ever since we first moved to town when I was only five years old. At first, we didn't spend much time together because our family lived on the south end of town and his family lived further north. Even so, his mother occasionally let him come over to our house to play. Later, when we moved into a larger home, we lived just kitty-corner from each other. By that time, we were old enough to roam at will around our small town. Every child in town was part of one gang that enjoyed playing together through all the varied seasons of the year.

9

From the first through the seventh grades, I was the only girl in my class. This came about because an illness kept my siblings and me at home during the first few months of the school year. The doctor quarantined our family for several months because Fritz became ill from scarlet fever. Before he recovered completely, Millie caught the fever. One by one, the five of us fell victim to this disease. When the doctor finally permitted us to go back to school, my teacher, Miss O'Keefe, had promoted the other girls in my class to the next grade because they were super intelligent and motivated learners. My wonderful teacher and I faced a classroom of boys. I was very happy in their company. I am not sure how my teacher felt about it.

As the memories continued and the miles flew by, I recalled the reason I had decided early on that I wanted to be a teacher. It happened when I was in the fifth grade. I had missed school again because I had the measles. When I returned to school, I had missed the classes in math that dealt with learning the value of Roman numerals. I had homework to catch up on and I had no idea what those numerals meant. I was frustrated to the point of tears. One of Lil's friends was visiting in our home when she noticed my distress. She kindly asked, "What is the matter? Can I help you?"

Bursting out in tears, I moaned, "I don't understand these damn Roman numerals."

Laughing, she comforted me, "Let me help you. They are very easy to understand. You will catch on quickly."

With much patience, she expertly explained the system and after several examples, the light bulb of understanding went on in my mind. I was amazed at her gift for teaching. It was then and there that I decided that I wanted to be a teacher when I grew up. Today I was on my way to realizing that dream.

Just then, the bus came to a halt and the driver called

out, "Valley Center."

I quickly gathered my belonging and as I proceeded to the exit, I saw a frail, little nun waiting to take me to my new home. My heart began to pound with excitement as I came nearer to that door of my future.

Chapter 2
Baffled and Bewildered

As I stepped down from the bus, this elderly nun introduced herself as Mother Gertrude. She spoke with a bit of a French accent. Like some of the nuns at boarding school, who still echoed traces of their native tongue in their speech, this nun's words did not really sound all that foreign to me.

I found out later that she was the Mother Superior of the whole convent setup here in America. She was subject to no other person except the Mother General who lived in France and who had authority over every nun in this particular international religious community. I also learned that when convent authority links the word "mother" with "superior," a definite pecking order is set up. Mother Superior, spokesperson for God, rules from the highest level over all nuns in her convent who are expected to obey without question.

However, right at this moment, I was unaware of her high level of authority. She was just another nun to me. I eagerly reached out my hand to greet her. She didn't seem to notice that gesture as she wordlessly beckoned me to follow her. Surprised by her manner, my smile slowly faded as I took a moment to adjust to this rather lukewarm welcome. I had expected a little more fanfare at my arrival. I wasn't expecting a marching band exactly but I had envisioned at least a small show of joy at meeting someone aspiring to be the perfect nun.

Shaken a bit by her formality, I grabbed my suitcase and ran to catch up with her. She may well have called herself Mother but this nun was certainly not anything like my own mother. My mother, Bessie, as we affectionately called her, was a furnace compared to this icebox of a nun.

Despite the snow covered roads and icy sidewalks, we swiftly covered the several blocks from the bus depot to the convent. She silently clipped along--with me always a few steps behind her. As I looked about this new town, I tried to take in whatever there was to see. Mother Gertrude, on the contrary, looked neither to the right nor to the left even when crossing a street. I wondered if traffic just stopped automatically when drivers saw a nun in their path! I decided to stick close to her with hopes that her "holy habit" would also protect me!

We did arrive safely at the convent, a large three-story brick building located on the same block as the Catholic Church with the parish rectory nestled in-between. We were careful to remove our snow-covered boots at the main entrance. We passed through the section of the building that housed both the elementary and the secondary levels of the school. Then Mother Gertrude guided me to the convent section, and finally to the room where two young girls, Anita and Margie, were waiting to greet me. To my surprise, Mother Gertrude introduced them as Sister Anita and Sister Margie. I thought that title would be a long time a-coming to me.

They were very friendly in their greetings. They both seemed excited to see me. Anita stepped forward first to squeeze my hand with her strong welcoming grip. Margie smiled shyly as she held my hand a bit longer than expected.

Anita had been with me in boarding school. In fact, when she had announced in the middle of our sophomore year that she was leaving to become a nun, wonder and admiration filled me. That was when the desire to become a nun started to develop.

When Mother Gertrude left us alone to attend to some other business, Anita smiled and said, "Hey, Grace, whatever makes you think you can be a nun? You were always just a little over the line with your mischief at school. You better believe you won't get by with your tricks here."

"If you can do it, I can too," I laughed. "This Mother Gertrude won't be in charge of us, will she?"

"You are wrong there," smiled Margie. "She is with us almost every hour of the day and she expects us to be very obedient to all her rules."

The first faint stirring of cowardly fear began to seep into my mind and heart. I looked around the room. There were no bars on the windows; there was nothing to prevent me from changing my mind at any time. However, it was not in my nature to give up so easily. Besides that, I sensed that my rising misgivings accurately measured my lack of trust in the Lord. I wanted no part of that. Even as I tried to disregard my doubts, my mother's voice rang out loud and clear in my memory, "Caution is never cowardice." I had thrown caution to the wind. Now it was up to me to give this life a fair trial. I must push through the inner whisperings that tried to tell me I was not worthy of such a high calling, that I probably would never pass the final tests and that I would wash out bringing shame upon my family.

Anita and Margie had entered the formation program several months before I came to the convent. After several enlightening discussions with them, their conversation proved they were still as clueless as I was concerning the full impact convent life would have on our lives.

I asked, "What have you been doing since you came here? Do you go to special classes?"

Anita took the lead by answering, "We have spent most of our time helping out in the kitchen because the cook has a lot of boarders to feed at every meal. I have peeled bushels of potatoes and prepared as many vegetables since I came here."

Margie added, "Mother Gertrude has been gone a lot to visit other convents so we haven't had a set schedule, but I think that is about to change."

I replied, "I could have stayed at boarding school for that. I had to work for my board and room there just like you did, Anita, when you were with me. You remember how we helped all around the convent: preparing vegetables, washing dishes, and shining hard wood floors. I expected something different here."

Recently, each of us had turned fifteen. We had asked for admittance to this religious community as provisional candidates. We (postulants, as we were called) admired the nuns and wished to serve God in what we thought was the best and quickest way to achieve a holy life.

As we continued to talk, we heard the approaching rhythmic click, click of Mother Gertrude's sturdy, determined steps as she returned from her errand. All conversation stopped as she briskly entered the room. Very soon, I began to see, that though she was tiny and somewhat frail looking, she was not a person with whom I wanted to tangle. As she set up our daily schedule, she said, "You are not to come late to any community exercises. I expect you to complete your daily chores with excellence and you will move through the halls quietly, without drawing attention to yourself."

Whoa! Margie was right. Things are about to change! Without a doubt, she means business!

With time, I also found her to be a very likable and dedicated woman. Although she was a native of France, she had lived here in the United States for many years. Her background in spirituality, culture, and communication was definitely Old World French. Had she been a sour, egotistical or belligerent person, I might have backed out of this situation from the beginning. She was none of these. She was a sweet, selfless and good-natured woman who took her calling very seriously.

After allowing me several days to become acquainted with my new surroundings, Mother called the three of us to begin our formation program. As we sat in the conference room assigned to us, Mother Gertrude looked us over with kindly, yet penetrating eyes. She spoke to us in a calm and confident manner, "Young ladies, you are here to learn to live a life totally different from what you have lived in the past. You have picked up many values from the world that are not fitting for a person who wants to serve the Lord. You may resent the stern discipline needed to transform you into worthy servants of the Lord."

When I cringed and looked to the others to see their reaction, Mother Gertrude's sharp eyes caught my response and immediately informed me that such a show of emotion was one example of my behavior that would have to change.

So, what was the problem for me? I just did not understand why she thought we were such badly formed Christians.

As she continued to explain what our training would be like, I began to understand the method that she would follow. Her task, it seemed to me, was to pour us into a mold that would turn out perfect nuns. When fully molded, we would then follow every rule of this religious community, and be fully prepared to go out into the world to bring others closer to God.

That made sense to me. I desired to bring others to know our loving God. However, I really didn't relish such a transformation that left me without the ability to question the reasons for this passive style of education.

In this nun's judgment, she faced an enormous task, something as formidable as "taking sows ears and turning them into silk purses." She set out to remake us, to squash the hold that the world had on us and to destroy our errant ways. Who in their right mind wants to go through such a procedure? Though those harsh words sounded ominous to me, I thought, *"Is such a process necessary to reach my goal of true holiness? Jesus poured out his life for me. I want to pour my life out for others too. Maybe I do need remaking."*

There were things my short life had already taught me that could stand some revision. One of my propensities is to beat around the bush whenever I face a situation that calls for simple, straightforward honesty. My first natural impulse is to dress up the truth or to attempt to sanitize it so that I don't look so horrific in a particular situation. My mother had done her best to train me to always tell the truth and to live a life of integrity, but she was not completely successful. Even when confessing, I always tried to find a word that would not sound so sinful.

Of course, there is that other penchant that impels me to leap into things for which I am ill prepared. In most cases, if any idea sounds good, I usually accept it without testing it through my own God-given intelligence. I often forget to seek the counsel provided by the Holy Spirit. My first reaction is "Full steam ahead! Gung ho!"

Regrets come later. I had yet to learn there is nothing positive about living with worthless regrets; such misgivings are a total waste of time if we learn nothing in the process. For the most part, I embraced convent discipline. Though I was far from perfect in my judgments, behavior and Christian awareness, I still puzzled at Mother Gertrude's obvious opinion of us.

While still at home, I had come to realize at the age of twelve that Jesus was asking for admittance into every corner of my heart. My mother had refused to let me go to a dance at a country school that all my classmates planned to attend. I became very angry when Mom said a definite, "No!" I left the room, slammed the door behind me, and retreated to the bedroom that I shared with Millie and Lil. There I pouted and indulged in a full-blown pity party. Out of the blue, the thought came to me that Mom was really just trying to protect me. I remembered all the times she had shown me so much love. I began to pray and at that moment, I realized that I was free to choose to be mean or obedient. Jesus was knocking at the door of my heart and I welcomed him in to be the Lord of my life. Then while attending boarding school at St. Benedict near Wild Rice, North Dakota, my religion teacher taught that every good Catholic must to be ready to present Jesus with a blank sheet of paper with his or her signature affixed at the bottom. This was a symbolic way of telling Jesus that he could write whatever he wanted on that paper because we trusted him completely. I had gone through that ritual so willingly. Between Jesus and me, our relationship had become very personal, yet very immature on my part. If I were to ask myself, "How many times have you sinned since making that first commitment?"--I would soon have lost count.

Thanks to my mother, I knew whenever I take matters into my own hands -- outside of God's will I sin. Still, Mom never wanted me to concentrate on sin. She focused on the peace that Jesus' forgiveness brings. My commitment to Jesus at age 12 did not miraculously change my personality. I still had bad tendencies that led me into trouble. My old self struggled against the new life that

Jesus gave me. I saw myself as a child of God, who *sometimes* sinned. Sin was certainly not my habitual style of life, as Mother Gertrude seemed to indicate.

There were times, even during my boarding school days, when I had to really forage around in my memory to find something to confess. Oh, there were childish pranks played; Dolly and I had smuggled fresh baked bread and spoonfuls of peanut butter out of the convent larder to treat our dormitory companions once a week on baking day. The nuns had compassionately turned a blind eye to those shenanigans. I had exchanged innocent kisses with my childhood boyfriends but that was as far as it went. I had smoked a few cigarettes and punished my taste buds with Coca Cola spiked with booze with my grade school companions on one occasion. I had hated the taste, spitting it out when my friends were not looking. That was the extent of my drinking days. Were those acts of mischief outrageous crimes? Was I really so hardened that I could not clearly see the malice hidden in my heart? Maybe I did not have what it takes to fill a holy nun vocation.

Chapter 3
Perplexed and Puzzled

My first months in the convent were very confusing and upsetting. I had expected some great transforming event to happen that would miraculously turn me into an instant saintly nun. Yet, everyday was filled with rigid rules of decorum rather than means of deepening my love of God. Along with that disappointment, I missed my family. At boarding school, I had overcome my homesickness very quickly, but here I constantly thought about my family. I gradually learned to adjust and to keep my disappointments stuffed down tightly inside. This unhealthy repression soon manifested itself in frequent, almost daily, migraine headaches that added an extra burden to this very difficult style of life. I failed to realize that I should have gone to Mother Gertrude to reveal my fears, doubts, and misgivings. I was foolish, young, and shy about going to a superior with my problems. Not yet schooled to listen to the Holy Spirit in every situation, I continued to make dim-witted choices.

Mother Gertrude warned us: "You must be obedient as your formation begins. You are not to question my directions or the rules. You must leave behind everything: your friends, your family, and all the bad habits that you acquired from your worldly contacts. All incoming and outgoing mail will be censored."

That last archaic regulation was not new to me; my days at the Catholic boarding school had prepared me to accept this exasperating rule. I had tried to find a way around it during my boarding school days, but now I knew there would be no chance for such tomfoolery here. Her opinions would have liked to isolate us entirely from our families, but evidently, she had rules to follow just as we did. Her expressed philosophy was that family ties only served to disrupt the order and discipline of community life. This philosophy was akin to the methods that my brothers had encountered in their military boot camp training.

Our dear Mother Superior continued her warnings; "You must see yourselves as part of a new family. You must look forward to strict discipline that is meant to weed out your obstinacy and willfulness."

"Holy Mother of God, there she goes again. I came here to fast track my journey to holiness. I never realized that I was such a sinful person. I wonder why my mother never pointed out my wickedness while I was at home. Even the nuns at the boarding school thought I was of good character."

Just then, in the middle of her stream of exhortations, my mind segued in another direction. Again, I humbly recalled that some of my childhood actions did need correction. In those situations, my mother always corrected in order to restore peace and harmony in our fun-loving boisterous family. She was careful not to humiliate or

22

degrade us.

There was that time when we (my parents and the youngest seven children of our family of ten) first moved to the little town of Verona, leaving the farm life behind us. As we became acquainted with the town folk, our mother allowed us to enjoy the freedom to come and go as we pleased, at least during the summer months. I was very young, but Mom trusted me to be polite and careful of other people's property. One day, I forgot all that when I spied something that my covetous little mind thought that I needed.

I was in Rickford's all-goods store where I saw a pair of pink anklets with delicate lace around the top. After looking around to see if anyone was watching me, I slipped the purloined parcel into my pocket. I was a shoplifter at age five! Arriving at home, I showed my ill-gotten goods to my mom. Raising her eyebrows and looking me square in the eye, she asked, "Where did you get them?"

"I was playing with Blythe Gaune, and her mother gave them to me."

She took me gently by the hand and said, "We need to thank her for such a nice gift."

Stammering and stuttering I gasped, "I did that already, Mom."

"Good for you! But now I want to give her my thanks too. That was very generous of her to give them to you. They really are very pretty, but you will have to wait to wear them because they are not really your size. They are much too big for you now."

With my head sinking lower and lower and my feet dragging with every step, we started our walk toward the Gaunes' home. Before we got very far, I finally gave up and told my mom the truth. We changed direction, and she took me to the store to return the stolen item. Mom had been calm but firm in her insistence on honesty.

Still, there were other occasions when that lesson on

integrity needed reinforcement. When my older brother, Ralph (better known as Sam) was still living at home, I stole a quarter from him and hid it among the leaves of a cabbage plant growing in our garden. It took Sam a long time to get the truth out of me, but I finally had to confess again. He said, "Grace, you will never make a good thief or a good liar." Maybe he was wrong, and I really was the great sinner that Mother Gertrude saw in me?

I quickly snapped out of my daydreams as Mother Superior's voice continued to ring out her list of rules and regulations. Her lectures were not especially riveting and I wondered how much I had missed as my mind had drifted to pleasant memories of home and my sweet mother, Bessie.

"You must always choose to do God's will," Mother Gertrude went on to say.

Timidly, I raised my hand to ask, "How will we know when our choices are God's will for us?"

She quickly answered, "That is a good question, Sister Grace. The answer to that is simple. From now on, you will find God's will in whatever I tell you to do. You must forget worldly pleasures. Your only pleasure will be to follow the wishes of those God has placed over you."

I concluded that meant I never again would I have to use my brain to figure things out, at least when trying to know the plan of God for me. Submitting to the "Holy Rule," her wishes and the routine of community life, ruled out the use of my own will. That meant no questions, challenges, disobedience, or hesitation could mark my responses in doing what my superiors asked of me. My mind numbed at the thought, *"You have enrolled in a school for robots! Now, why should you complain? You entered in this school of own free choice. Live with it!"*

"There's no need to fear the wind, if all your haystacks are tied down," as many a good Irish person would say in such a situation.

Later that day, to prove to myself the sincerity of my dedication and to place more secure binders on my emotional haystacks, I took out the photo of my childhood sweetheart, Dick Taylor. I had hidden his picture among the few things that I had brought with me. Mother Gertrude had recommended that besides leaving behind our family, we must also forget the boys with whom "we had sinned."

I had skated, danced, biked, smooched, and skirted the boarding house rules a bit in my juvenile relationship with Dick, but none of those things were sins in my mind. Nevertheless, I was determined to become the perfect nun. Slowly, with great feelings of heroism, I tore Dick's picture into tiny shreds and flushed them down the toilet. I was confident that I was progressing nicely on my way to sainthood!

It was a passionate, yet reasonable juvenile reaction to ideas presented by someone I assumed was speaking for God. I decided to be very submissive and obedient. I figured I could do it, no matter how hard it would get. It did get more and more difficult as time went on. Many more surprising days were just around the corner.

Because Mother Gertrude put great emphasis on keeping rules, a nervous "worry-bug" began to infect my soul. Rule keeping was not my long suit and yet that direction seemed linked to the degree of holiness that I wanted to achieve. In fact, at this point, I was not at all sure that I had any real idea of what holiness meant except that I wanted to be a follower of Jesus. What he wanted, I wanted. I remembered Jesus' words to Martha: "One thing is needful. Mary has chosen the good portion…" I believed that portion was making that connection with Jesus and with what he wants our lives to be.

Did Jesus' call to holiness mean observing every rule? What did walking sedately up the stairs, keeping my eyes downcast, avoiding people from the outside, not having any 'particular friendships,' concealing my hands and arms in my sleeves, and a myriad of other regulations have to do with what Jesus wants from my life?

It was all so puzzling and not all that fulfilling. Jesus promised peace to those who accepted his teaching. My days and nights were not exactly peaceful.

As I studied Jesus and his way, it seemed to me that his words proclaimed more about relationships than perfection. He asked for a commitment to his way of love, mercy and forgiveness in our everyday lives. *Did he want me stressed out in my striving to please him by keeping all the rules?* The daily results of that produced shame and frustration-- not joy in his service.

I worried that I was really missing the mark in so many ways, though in my saner moments, I also knew that Jesus would not expect me to be a mature person in even a few years' time. Maturity would be a long way down my path. Father Devor, the convent chaplain, could attest to that because of an incident that proved this point. It concerned my misunderstanding of the real meaning of the Eucharist.

My training at the age of seven for First Communion, under the tutelage of the nuns who came to our parish for just two weeks every summer, centered on testing my ability to distinguish ordinary bread from the bread that Jesus gives us as his Body and Blood. The nuns also emphasized exterior rituals: folding of the hands on the way up the aisle, not letting the host touch our teeth, and holding up the communion cloth draped over the communion rail so that not a crumb from the host would be spilled on the floor.

While at home, I had never been one to worry over ritualism. We attended Mass every Sunday, but it was out of love and not from a sense of duty. Yet, here in the convent, with so much emphasis put upon rules and regulations, my understanding of these external rituals led me to fret excessively, at least about the following incident.

One morning, after receiving the host, I sneezed

unexpectedly. I thought I saw a piece of the host fly from my mouth but I couldn't see where it landed. Extreme worry assailed me. Somehow, I felt responsible if somebody stepped on it or otherwise dishonored it. After Mass, I went with a quaking heart and my upsetting qualms to consult with Father Devor.

So frightened by this incident, when I explained the situation to Father, I hedged (lied outright) by making him believe that someone had come to me with this worry, and I didn't know how to advise that person.

As soon as my pathetic story gushed from my panicky mouth, I was sure that this gentle priest saw right through my deception. But he compassionately allowed that ruse to slip by without comment. Instead, he proceeded to assure me that to worry was more of an offense to the Lord's goodness than any dishonor this "sneezer" could have committed. He must have seen the enormous relief that came upon me with that news. He continued to assure me that the most important part of receiving communion deals with a loving and repentant heart eager to surrender oneself to the Lord. He said, "When you receive the host, offer yourself to be broken and shared with others who need you, just as Jesus did with his life. Your Amen should mean, 'I'm staking my life on giving as Jesus gave and knowing that his death and resurrection give me the assurance of his merciful presence."

Finally, this wise priest said, "You tell the one who sneezed that each person's thoughts should be centered on what Christ has done for us and not on a rule that only serves to make a person worry. Christ came to bring peace, not worry." And then the good priest winked at me. I knew he knew! Indeed, I had a long way to go to reach the understanding needed to live convent life honestly and effectively.

As the days of the first months in the convent slipped by, I continued to ponder the wisdom of my choice.

Looking back on all these experiences, I believe this community used some of the same methods that the military uses to indoctrinate and train its soldiers. They were testing us to see just how sincere we were in our commitment to serve the Lord. I would continue to wonder about a lot of things, but for the most part, I did comply with all attempts to purify my character.

Chapter 4
Repressed and Restrained

Each of my convent days began at what I considered an "ungodly" hour, 5:00 a.m. At the clanging of a loud bell, we arose from our beds with their thin, lumpy mattresses. Heavy white curtains separated our tiny cells, giving us a modicum of privacy. However, these cloth partitions were not thick enough to shut out the sounds that naturally arise from closely confined bodies. Alas, I found out that nuns could snore and effluviate just like the rest of the human race. I had tried to hold in every un-nun-like bodily emission that ached to escape. I even tried to suppress my sneezes, fearing that, too, was taboo. It was a miracle that I never "blew my top" or my bottom with those misconceptions of what is proper decorum for a nun. It is safe to say I was "nun"-plused about many things.

In the weak light of the dormitory, we hastily took turns washing at one of the five porcelain sinks lined up along one wall. Then we hurriedly dressed to arrive in the chapel by 5:30. There, one of the nuns took her turn reading morning prayers in French. They never varied in their rigid format. Public spontaneous prayer was virtually unknown. We each had a copy of the prayers, but I understood only a few words.

After that morning ritual, everyone sat down in the quiet chapel, always kept dim to conserve electricity, as Mother Superior read aloud from a French book on some subject for meditation. We, to whom French was still all-too foreign, read from books in English. The content was intended to inspire us to become more obedient, docile, and therefore, holier. Without fail, before ten minutes of the hour had passed, my head was bobbing up and down as I fell in and out of sleep. Mother Gertrude admonished me morning after morning. Each morning, I firmly resolved to sit up straight and pay attention. Mother finally threw up her hands and categorized me as incorrigible. My spirit was willing but my flesh was weak at that time of the morning. A wise solution might have allowed me sleep a little longer rather than risk breaking my neck as my head snapped up and down in my efforts to stay alert.

In the hour between Morning Prayer and the celebration of Mass, we completed an assigned job, either cleaning the stairs or helping in the kitchen to prepare breakfast for the boarders. There were many beautiful, well-waxed hardwood steps in this three-story high building. They were always polished and shining no matter how heavy the traffic. Often my chore was to sweep the outdoor stairs. I loved that job because it got me outside where I could let the wonderful fresh air energize my sleepy head. After Mass, we had other cleaning chores, studies to complete, and prayers to recite. Day by day, we progressed as we studied the list of rules and became more decorous in our outward behavior.

Despite the convent's rigid protocol, Anita, Margie, and

I became good friends though we had somewhat different personalities. Few things arose that bothered Anita's practical and realistic nature. She was determined to use her life to be of service to others. She was not a stickler for the rules, but she didn't go out of her way to break them either. If they served her purpose, it was well and good. If she had to bend the rules a bit to be of help to someone, she never hesitated to look to the spirit of the rule rather than the strict letter of the law. I admired her maturity. I had trouble discerning when to go beyond the rules, though I often did do just that.

Margie was a little harder to fathom. She loved to laugh and joke, but there were times when her melancholic nature caused her to withdraw from us. For no apparent reason, she might become dejected and depressed. Any attempts Anita and I made to restore her to a more cheerful disposition were often futile. When the dark clouds passed, she never seemed to remember that she had been in low spirits.

Both Anita and Margie looked to me for entertainment. When I put on my rose-colored glasses in my need for some comic relief, they welcomed my attempts to introduce any outlandish farcical interlude in our solemn, mundane, and often-humdrum routine. Despite my limited repertoire, I usually came up with something that caused a bit of amusement. The trick lay in the timing so Mother Gertrude did not witness it. Hypocrisy and I became bosom buddies. I learned to present a serious behavior in her presence and a frivolous one in the company of my friends.

As part of our formation program, we were to continue our high school education. That process turned out to be quite a travesty and a sad source of disillusionment.

Mother Superior allowed us to take one class in American History with Sister Zelda who taught the sophomore students. We did not enter her actual classroom where the other students might taint us with worldly ideas.

We listened to Sister Zelda's lectures from a little room off the main classroom. There was a small opening just high enough in the wall to prevent us from seeing our teacher or any of the students. It did allow the sound of her voice to come through to us, but that was not all.

Sister Zelda, a great historian, was legally blind. As might be expected, her classroom discipline was virtually nonexistent. Sister's method of teaching was solely by lecture. She was never, in the least degree, aware of the boys in that class who routinely stood on their desks and peered at us through that small opening in the wall. They took turns standing there, vying for our attention and flirting outrageously with us. We tried to ignore them as we sat obediently listening and taking notes from Sister Zelda's insightful lectures. For some reason, Mother Gertrude had always left us unsupervised in that tiny room. Neither she nor Sister Zelda ever heard from us about the terrible chaos that went on in that room. Nevertheless, I did learn some history, a favorite subject, in what was purportedly the second half of my sophomore year.

Mother Gertrude cautioned us not to have any contact whatsoever with the other students. She taught us a difficult convent practice called "modesty of the eyes." A good nun acquires this virtue by keeping her eyes downcast as much as possible. I tried to practice this virtue but I still could not help but notice those good-looking lads who found it such great sport to flirt with "nuns in the making." Little did I know that in just a couple of years, I would be back in this same school, teaching boys who were only slightly younger than my age.

Mother also strictly forbade friendships of any kind even among the members of the community. Those kinds of friendships were "particular friendships," insinuating they were "not nice." It took me quite a long time to understand just what that phrase meant in practical terms. I knew that Jesus had friends while he was on earth:

choosing Peter, James and John as his particular friends. Of course, he was God, and he could withstand any evil temptations that Mother Gertrude seemed to imply were inherent in all such friendships. This concept was indeed very alien to my way of thinking. I loved to have fun, play innocent tricks on my companions, and serve up mischief any chance I got. In my dealings with my friends, I never experienced any unsavory attraction that might lead to something horrendously sinful.

Even though we had strict rules of silence during the day and night, I could not resist disregarding some rules from time to time. Bounding up the stairs, two or three steps at a time with youthful vitality, relating innocent jokes, or jumping out from behind doors to scare Anita or Margie seemed blameless and entertaining. Mature nuns considered these acts "unbecoming levity." Such lightheartedness was contrary to this straight-laced convent's standards. However, Anita and Margie were good sports. They never snitched on me about my many infractions of the rules, though tradition encouraged us to inform on each other for the good of community living.

Even if nobody snitched on our "sinful" ways, we were never "home free;" we had to accuse ourselves in a monthly event called "the chapter of faults." On the last Sunday of every month, the community made a deep silent retreat from their ordinary life that never was very boisterous in my estimation. After the Sunday Mass, everything was in solemn silence. Each nun spent her time, not in necessary or helpful activities like correcting papers, planning classroom lessons, studying assigned school subjects, or reading a good novel. Instead, they spent hours in the chapel, praying, meditating, examining their consciences, and reading inspirational treatises. Meanwhile, Mother Superior was in her office, privately receiving the nuns one by one.

We postulants became acquainted with this self-incriminating procedure early in our training. We learned to humbly enter her chambers, kneel in front of her chair, and confess all infractions of the rules that we had made during the past month. Her usually placid face would take on a more severe expression, set and determined, as she would instruct us about correcting our evil ways. Then she would impose a penance like kneeling during meals for a specified number of days. (You won't believe the number of meals I ate assuming that posture of repentance.) After questioning us about our spiritual progress, measured for the most part by our adherence to the rules, she sent us on our way to continue in prayer.

As a child, I had thought confessing to a priest was difficult; this was definitely far worse. When confessing real sins to a priest, I, at least, had the consolation of believing that he had the power to assure me that God forgives my sins. I thought that Mother Superior had no such power and was only training me to be submissive in the presence of her authority.

After Mother Superior had interviewed all the nuns, the chimes rang out and we advanced to the dining hall where we knelt, waiting silently for her arrival. She led us in formal prayer and then each nun in turn would bow low, kiss the floor in humility, and accuse herself aloud of her most grievous public faults. If anyone wished, they could accuse the confessing nun of any faults that she had failed to mention. Satan must have invented this practice. I believe it originated there and should have remained there! I hated and dreaded those last Sundays of the month. Obediently, I tried to put all these unholy thoughts aside but they were always there, boiling on the back burner of my mind. I was really having a very hard time attaining my much-desired degree of holiness. My halo was fading and dull; it seemed to grow dimmer each day.

Since the community had an extreme shortage of classroom teachers, they relentlessly pushed us through high school. Our records held many credits that we never earned in the usual sense. Because we helped with the tasks of keeping that large school and convent clean, this activity went on record as credits in "Home Economics." We earned like citations in many subjects taught by invisible teachers. Among these bogus credits, French grossed many points. Mother Superior felt justified in this appropriation because we listened to hours of community prayers recited in that language. These were great lessons in learning the art of rationalization, though those credits never appeared on our account!

It is true that I did know some French. I had started to learn that beautiful language at boarding school in my first year attending St. Benedict Catholic High School. Then I went on to second year French before entering the convent. However, the formal study of French halted in my studies in the convent because that was "secular" learning as opposed to "spiritual" knowledge.

Besides our non-lessons in French, we did study a whitewashed version of Church History. We read about the lives of the Saints and studied a little bit of the Bible. That was the extent of my schooling during my sophomore year. There were no science, math, English, literature, or social studies classes. Nevertheless, these subjects appeared magically on my high school records. The lessons my mother had taught me about integrity were definitely at war with many things that I witnessed in the convent. I dared not voice my objections to any of this. I was to obey without question!

Postulant training was usually completed in six months, but because of our youth and our frisky personalities, Mother Gertrude decided that we needed a full year of cleansing before we would be allowed to proceed to the Novitiate training in Autumn Vale, Illinois.

There were many days when all I wanted to do was call home and ask my parents to rescue me from this purgatory on earth. On other days, I was convinced that this was God's will for me. I still had a deep desire to share God's love with the whole world. None of that enthusiasm had dimmed, but it was no longer clear to me how many of the things that I was learning had anything to do with my hallowed dreams.

It would be many years before I realized that these dear nuns had acquired a few false notions about the Christian life. In France, where this community started, a widespread Jansenistic movement taught people some self-loathing practices that did not conform to true Christian principles. This false teaching stressed the idea that we are totally unworthy to approach God. It disallowed frequent communion. When a wretched soul did desire to receive this sacrament, the confession of sins must always precede it. It further declared: "You need to live a good life, deny yourself pleasure, and follow all prescribed rules and regulations to the letter. The more you suffer, the more holy you become." This was the recipe for making one pleasing to God, which placed one on the true path to holiness. Those ideas lead a person to believe that one had to get oneself clean before one can approach God. However, Jesus taught that we come to him just as we are and he will clean us up. We are not capable of cleaning up on our own no matter how hard we try.

The church finally condemned this teaching but once an error etches itself into a lifestyle, it is very hard to shake off in daily practice and thinking. Pleasing God, based on performance rather than on his goodness, ultimately leads to discouragement, sometimes to scruples, and always to feelings of unworthiness. It took many years for me to realize that attaining holiness was not my job and not my calling. Looking on it as my work focused my attention on myself. Self-centeredness never brings happiness or holiness. My holiness is God's work as a gift of his life working in me.

And so, my life continued with all its usual ups and downs. Some days went smoothly and others progressed with some difficulties. On one of those thorny days, Mother Gertrude came up with what she thought was a brilliant idea. One of the nuns, Sister Albertine, was a very talented musician. Whenever she played the organ in the parish church, her music swept me up to heavenly realms. Mother Gertrude thought that I should take piano lessons from this brilliant nun so that someday I could teach others. *Lord, preserve me!*

While I was still living at home, a neighbor lady had attempted to teach me piano lessons. I learned to read notes and I could play simple pieces in a flat mechanical way. I loved all kinds of music and appreciated that wonderful gift in others. Some members of my family had musical talent, but by the time it came down to me, I think that God had given most of that endowment to the eight siblings who had come before me. My mother, Bessie, had a rich alto voice and she had taught herself how to play the piano. She and my sister, Lil, sang in the choir. At home, when their voices blended on "Oh, Danny Boy," and Mom's nimble fingers rippled through those rich notes, we listened and applauded as they sang. At times, Mildred and Gene could easily join in with their good voices, but whenever I tried, Lil tried to stick her elbow in my mouth to block out the discordant squawks that inevitably screeched out of my dissonant vocal chords.

What a nightmare it must have been for Sister Albertine to listen to my murderous rendition of pieces like the "Turkish March." My prayer: *"Please God, don't ask me to teach piano. You know that you have not given me that gift. No matter how much I practice, my fingers just don't obey the music scores in front of me. I give up, dear Lord. You have to take it from here."*

"Do you mean that? Really? Are you going to trust that I am in control?" Although I could not hear God's voice, as usual, God must have chuckled over his plans for me. Through the silly choices of others, he would accomplish surprising things with my acknowledged incompetence. If I had been listening, he must have said, "Sorry, Grace, but no, you will be teaching music in the sweet by and by, and I will be there to help you."

I am so glad that I could not see into the future. There, God's great sense of humor, timing, and planning would have shocked me. When we give up our inept ways to him, he works unencumbered by our efforts that see only through our narrow-minded visions. He came to heal the broken-hearted, which includes all the ways we humans have of messing up our lives. I came to learn to turn over to Jesus all of the things that I did not know how to do. He supported my weaknesses with his strength.

When the school term ended in the spring, we spent most of our time scrubbing, waxing, dusting, painting, and helping the nuns polish everything in and outside of the school until everything sparkled. Mr. Clean might have fit right in if only he had not been male.

This "vacation" time was more relaxing because there were no students from whom we had to be isolated. Most of the teachers worked side-by-side with us. They ignored the rules of silence and surprised us with their wonderful humor and understanding of our difficulties in adjusting to this rigorous life. In my head, I wasn't sure they should be disobeying the rules like they were, but in my heart, I knew it was right. I thought that if Jesus had been there with us, he would have been laughing and joking along with us. It was a good time!

Chapter 5

Reprieve & Regression

That summer of 1946, after we had scoured most of the school and convent until it passed meticulous inspection, Mother Gertrude told us that we were going to spend a couple of weeks in Lystrom, North Dakota with an elderly nun, Sister Louise. All the teachers in that school were leaving to teach catechism in parishes throughout the diocese of Fargo that had no Catholic school for children to learn the basics of Catholic belief. Sister Louise was the cook and housekeeper in that school and she did not want to stay alone while the teachers were gone.

Sister Louise was a tiny French nun with a face as wrinkled as a prune. She was jolly and we felt comfortable spending time with her. For a very pleasant change, it was great to be free of Mother Gertrude's ever-watchful eye and to stop scouring dirt from every corner of the school.

We went with Sister Louise on long walks around the

little town. We were pleased when we stopped by a little shop where she purchased ice cream cones for us on some occasions. It seemed as though everyone knew Sister Louise. Men and women came out of their houses to greet her as we walked by. They often invited us into their homes where they treated us with cold drinks and sweets. Sister Louise was never in such a hurry that we couldn't take time to visit. She evidently did not believe that we had to be isolated from the people of this town.

Each day, we attended "Holy Hour" in the school chapel with the parish priest, Father O'Donal. He told me that I was in charge of starting the hymns that he expected to use in this hour of worship.

"Father, I don't have a very good voice for singing. I will be off-key for sure," I dared to contend.

"You just go ahead. We will join in to help you," he directed.

He was a tough Irish priest who found humor in everything, even in making a young girl squirm because of her ineptness.

After he led an opening prayer, I nervously tried to intone the specified hymn. Some kind of a croak issued from my throat. The other two postulants, Sister Louise, and Father began to laugh until the tears were rolling down their cheeks. Not wanting to be a poor sport, I joined in. When we again gained control of ourselves, Father told me to try again.

A little bird had come to rest on the chapel window ledge. She cocked her little head as if waiting for me to start. I tried again to sound the correct beginning note. As soon as my off-tune refrain emerged from my nervous throat, the little bird flew off in a fluttering panic. Father O'Donal declared in his heavy Irish brogue, "And to be sure, even the birds know you can't carry a simple tune."

After everyone had again stopped laughing, I said, "Father, I'm done. If you can do better, you can start the hymns yourself."

"To be sure, your voice is not much to boast about. The good Lord will not miss out on much if we continue in blessed silence," he chuckled. Our prayer service continued without worship hymns at all after that debacle.

After our all too-short stay with Sister Louise, we returned to Valley Center and to the tasks that awaited our homecoming.

For ordinary days, we wore long dresses made of heavy serge cloth, but when we worked at messy cleaning tasks, we wore a lighter, black gabardine robe. No matter, these "holy habits" were so very cumbersome. When no outsiders were around, the nuns hitched up their long skirts and pinned them loosely between their legs. They literally "girded up their loins." We postulants thought that sight bordered on the ridiculous. Soon, however, we followed suit when we found that it did facilitate our labors.

Over this garb, we wore a small cape that extended to our waists. The purpose of this cape was to conceal our girlish breasts. Mother Gertrude did not allow us to wear any kind of bra. She considered such unmentionables too worldly for nuns. I was always very embarrassed about my ample boobs just hanging loose but I learned to say, "Ainsi soit-il," (Amen) even to that.

One day a nun from Wild Rice, Sister Agnes, came to Valley Center. She had been in charge of us when we were in the dorm at school. Mother Gertrude gave us permission to accompany her on a walk. I had always greatly admired this lovely nun. She was beautiful in body, soul and spirit. Now I felt even more at ease with her. She was a welcome relief from some of the sterner nuns. Arriving back at the convent and seeing no one around, she playfully suggested we have a race down one of the long halls in the school.

Gladly we took up the challenge as we tore through the hall and up the stairs to the high school classrooms. Reaching the top, we were laughing, breathless, and having a good time with this simple amusement. Sister cautioned us to hurriedly regain our composure because otherwise someone might think we were "dissipated." Feigning ignorance of the meaning of that word, (indulgence in the intemperate pursuit of pleasure), I innocently asked her if that meant the opposite of constipated. She burst out laughing. After a few more minutes of easy banter, she told us it was time for her to leave for Wild Rice and her duties at my old boarding school. She reached out to hug each of us before departing on her way.

She had not foisted on us that strange French convent custom of "chin-rubbing," we had often seen exchanged between departing and arriving nuns. It was a weird substitute for a kiss. Much like the Eskimo custom of rubbing noses to avoid lips freezing from the cold, the nuns had a good reason for this bizarre practice. This custom came about because the headdress, made of a fragile starched cloth, protruded so far out from the face that the only way to exchange a "kiss" was to stick out chins and rub them.

After her departure, I felt a deep loneliness for home. Mother Gertrude noticed it and told me that my mother had written to her, insisting that I return home because she knew that I was far too young to know the seriousness of what I was doing. I wanted to know how she answered my mother's plea. She replied, "I simply told your mother that she must not interfere with God's will."

She had used her spiritual authority as a weapon to subdue my mother, who highly regarded the opinions of nuns and priests. Their voices came across to her as strong as the words of the Bible: "Thus sayeth the Lord."

Mother Gertrude added that she had reminded my mother that if I had stayed at home, I might have become pregnant out of wedlock. In such a scenario, she assumed that Mom would not have insisted that I stay at home until I grew up but would have demanded that I marry immediately.

*You don't know anything about my mother! You have
no idea what she might have done in such a situation. You
had no right to tell her what was right or wrong!*

I was angry at her assumptions but I dared not express
my thoughts to her. She must have completely intimidated
my mother with her arguments because Mom never shared
with me anything about this correspondence between them.
When I learned of it, I was deeply chagrined. Here would
have been a justifiable escape hatch. If I had known of my
mother's deep concerns, I think that I would have gladly
returned to civilian life. Then again, maybe not!

All during this probation period, we knew little or
nothing about news items. However, we did hear some of
the students talk about the atomic bombing of two cities,
Hiroshima and Nagasaki, in Japan. They talked excitedly
about how a B-29 plane, the *Enola Gay* had dropped the
first bomb called *Little Boy* and the second one named *Fat
Man* and of the terrible ravages these bombs spread on
those Japanese cities. We also heard that the Japanese
surrendered on August 14 of that year. The war in Europe
ended in May, 1945. My brothers would soon be coming
home from their military service.

Meanwhile, after almost a full year of training, the
superiors admitted us as novices in the community. We had
passed the first probationary period in our formation.

On January 25, 1946, at the age of 16, I received my
new name, Sister Monica Rose, and my new attire, the
formal robes of a real nun from the hands of the Bishop in a
solemn ceremony. This also included the cutting of my hair
to symbolize giving up the vanities of the world. All of
these changes signified we were to be completely dead to
our old lives as we began the next step in our formation.

My parents came to be with me at this ceremony that marked an important milestone in my life. I was so excited; more about seeing my parents than about the upcoming ceremony.

The day was a very stormy one, and I was afraid my parents would not be able to make it, but Dad was able to maneuver his way through forty miles of blowing snow.

Mother Gertrude allowed me to go home for one day and she even allowed me to stay overnight since the weather was so very unsettled. I was so thrilled that I hardly noticed the miles slip by as Dad cautiously made his way over the roads with the snow blowing drifts in many places. All of my siblings were going to be at home to greet me. My parents had asked them all to come home so that we could have our family picture taken the next day. Upon reaching our home and coming into our house, I was overwhelmed with the joy of seeing their faces after so long a time. Gene and Fritz were the first to greet me. I could tell they weren't sure how to go about this; they finally just slapped me on the back and said, "Welcome home, Sis!

Aggie, Mary and Lil had a delicious meal ready and they soon insisted that we sit down to eat before the food became overcooked. Everyone started talking at once and soon the house resounded with laughter, questions, and sharing of stories. What a delight is was to be with my family again!

Book Two
A Radically Rattled Rookie

*Each must do what is asked, without sadness or compulsion,
for God loves a cheerful giver.*
2COR 9:7

I have learned from experience that the greater part of our happiness or misery depends upon our dispositions, and not upon our circumstances.
Martha Washington (1732-1802)

Chapter 6
To Be or Not to Be

Soon after my return to the convent from my home visit, we prepared to travel by train to Illinois to the convent-training center, the Novitiate. We were no longer postulants but novices now that we had passed the first phase of our formation and had taken on a new name. Our new dresses (habits) were different also. They were very much like those of fully professed nuns except we wore white veils over our coifs rather than a black veil.

It is surprising to me that while I can recall so vividly the many memories of my childhood, this period of my life seems barren by comparison. I know that I was much less sure of myself facing this second probationary period than I had been facing the first. Doubts plagued me as each day presented trying circumstances that brought out a longing to see more clearly God's plan for me.

In the middle of my sophomore year, when I had the

left the Catholic boarding school to enter the convent, I had done so without much serious thought. I had consulted no one. With about as much stability as a fluttering butterfly, I ignored the warnings of my siblings and the advice of my mother, who was well aware of my immaturity.

I had learned from my Baltimore Catechism that when I was baptized, the water symbolized that my old life had been washed away because the faith of my family spoke for me. Jesus had won the battle over sin and death. Sin had no more control over me as I continued to walk with the Lord. I was a child of God, nurtured in faith by my Christian family.

At an early age, when I became more aware of what some of that meant, I had chosen to let Jesus work out his salvation in me. I struggled with the convent's idea that now somehow I had to die all over again. That concept was not totally wrong. God does call us to surrender, to trust in him, and to heed the guidance of the Holy Spirit. That is what I had not yet learned to do. I had not learned to discern his counsel that comes from the wisdom of legitimate authority or from his private whispered message heard deep in my heart.

It was only much later in life that I learned that God is, in no way, obliged to finish what He did not start in the first place. Even now, I cannot say with certainty that God called me to convent life or if that was just a noble idea that I cooked up on my own. Regretfully, nuns and the clergy were always placed in a level above common believers. I still firmly believe in God's divine providence. After we have made a mess of things by our choices, he is right there to help us make something of any situation in which we place ourselves. I had to learn this repeatedly, and still do-- even to this day.

My mother passed on to me her belief that God has a plan for each of us. Through life, we constantly make free choices. That is what separates us from the animal world.

Additionally, she taught me that we have to face the natural consequences of those choices. As children of God, we can be sure that God is with us, even in our most immature, foolish, and even sinful choices. No matter how dumb we act, God is ever at work within us to separate our sinfulness from our righteousness in him. He helps us see how to make the most of even a very bad situation. Even if our life is filled with a comedy of errors, God will see us through, stepping aside when we make bad choices, but ever ready to help the moment we call upon him, and admit our willfulness. He shows us his way. His way may not be according to our time, plan, or what we had envisioned, but rest assured, his way will always prevail. As my mother often told me, "God can write straight with crooked lines. Whatever Satan means for harm, God uses for our good."

Whatever compelled me to make the choices I did, those choices would change my life and would point me down a path where I found some folly and some wisdom. The folly centered mostly on my inability to question things and to speak up about things that I didn't understand. For example, I did not understand why superiors thought they had the right to open our personal mail, why we were not permitted more family contacts and why we had so little time to relax and enjoy life. The wisdom part came from the gift of prayer that the Lord opened up to me. Prayer carried me through many difficult times. If I could have seen how long that path extended, I am sure that I would not have had the courage to forge ahead. Actually, I did not really *forge* ahead. A better description of the manner of my journey would be that I muddled my way through, dealing with doubts and misgivings along the way.

As I began this second stage of convent training, I knew it would be more of the same experiences as I had in the postulate, except that it would be more rigorous. At least that is what Mother Gertrude forewarned, as we were about to leave for the Novitiate.

To reach our destination, we boarded the train from Valley Center. (The days of nun-driven cars had not yet evolved as an accepted mode of travel in our community.) Since we arrived during winter, the soggy humid days of typical Illinois summers were yet to be experienced. Still, for me, Illinois was somewhat foreign, as previously I had rarely left the boundaries of North Dakota.

Our housing was in an isolated section of a huge building complex (huge--at least from my rural-oriented view) known as St. Magdalene's Hospital, Convent, and Novitiate in Autumn Vale, Illinois. Many of the resident nuns would play a significant part in my life during the next two and a half years.

One of these was the nun in charge of our training, Mother Mary Edwin. She was American-born (of French descent, however), blessed with a good deal of common sense, and a great sense of humor. She was a welcome relief from what we had undergone under the foreign-slanted tutelage of Mother Gertrude. This lady was just as resolute in her task of turning out good nuns but she did not attempt to pour each of us into a uniform mold by crushing and breaking us. She made allowances for our unique personalities. She took care to match our gifts and talents to the tasks that she assigned. She never made me feel like a beggar when I needed to ask for a remedy for my headaches. She was also very solicitous about our health in every area. Her training was far more gentle and humane, a welcome respite in this new environment.

At the most inopportune times, I began to have thoughts about the high school experiences I missed by rushing headlong into the convent. Popular hit tunes I once listened to at home began playing in the echoes of my mind. Even though they didn't mean much to me before, holding on to them now seemed crucial to my sanity. There was still limited freedom to make friends, share our feelings and spend time just fooling around.

As we continued to have morning prayers in French, it was even harder to concentrate, when such tunes as "Jeepers Creepers," "O Johnny, O Johnny," the memorable "Flat Foot Floogie" or "I'm Forever Blowing Bubbles" kept up their devilish repetitions in competition with my morning meditations.

In this somewhat warmer and more humid climate of Illinois, I often wished that we didn't have to wear such heavy clothing that seemed to smother me in more ways than one. Still I wavered from day to day between my desire to serve God as a nun and my growing awareness that this way might not really be His way.

Finally, I decided that I could not keep waffling back and forth in my resolution to stay or leave. I saw that it was not healthy to keep entertaining daydreams of returning home where I could honestly earn my high school diploma, live in a normal family atmosphere, and seek Godly service in some other simpler way. I knew that a dissatisfied person is frustrated, hard to get along with, and would not be a good witness to the goodness of God. I certainly didn't want to become a sour, crabby, joy-killing nun. I did not want anyone to look at me and say, "If that's what it's like to be a Christian, then I want no part of it."

I wanted to show by my life that God's way was the only way to true happiness and peace. I finally realized the source of most of my conflicts: I was concentrating on all the negative things in my life. I realized that a life filled with a long list of "don'ts" is bound to kill joy. Jesus was always positive in all his teachings. Love, hope, joy, confidence, and forgiveness were the hallmarks of his life. I knew my only choice was to take up a different mind-set. I would choose life! I would concentrate on the wonders of God's love for me and ignore everything negative. I wanted him to give me strength. I trusted him no matter how much effort the circumstances of each day required. I was again full of zeal. I did not want to be a lamp with a burned-out bulb. I began to embrace this life, determined to be the best nun that I could be with the gifts that God had given me. I would stay in this race to the end. I was in it for the long haul. I would do everything with my whole heart. I would not be lukewarm and compromising. Alas! It was not that easy to keep my wonderful resolutions. My focus on good things often wavered, but I learned to "whistle a happy tune" and go on. (Silently, of course!)

Chapter 7
Settling In

The three of us who had just come from North Dakota met with our new companions. Sister Bernadine (formerly Margie), Sister Francine (formerly Anita), and I joined a larger group of probationary nuns who had entered at least a year and a half before we had. They were now near the end of their "canonical year," the year that would prepare them to take their first vows. Another group was just beginning their canonical year. Thus, we had to learn to interact with several new personalities.

Sister Elisa, Sister Rachyl, and Sister Ann were three of the older girls who had entered before the three of us. They were our models as they were nearly ready to make temporary vows. They had all entered from the same town of Harwell, North Dakota. They were very different from one another. All three followed the rules very closely but to different degrees and perhaps from different motives.

Elisa's mother had died when she was very young and Elisa had raised her younger siblings. She was older and very mature in her ways. She seemed to be perfect in everything she did. When she knelt for the "Chapter of Faults" each month, nobody ever accused her of having broken any rules. Sister Rachyl was a comic, a little moody, but generally free and full of fun. Sister Ann was harder to figure out because she often shifted her opinions in our discussions without any pattern. It was impossible to know exactly where she stood at any given moment. She was quick about her tasks, always done well and in a good spirit. Each of these companions were much more mature than I ever hoped to be. We all got along. I tried to be a good example, but I was still very immature, ready to play more often than to be serious. I am glad the others had better models to lead them.

One day a young lady, Lorrie, joined our group as a postulant. She was a marvel. On the first night after her entrance, a terrible rainstorm erupted during the early evening hours. The thunder was deafening with the lightening lighting up the whole sky and the wind driving the rain against the buildings so fiercely that several windows blew open. The rain poured through the screens in torrents. I remember standing there, scared and shaken by the storm that echoed through the deep ravines on the north side of the convent.

Lorrie had been with us just one day, yet she had the presence of mind to know exactly what to do. She had observed where the cleaning materials were housed on her tour through the convent. She rushed down the stairs, grabbed all that was necessary to mop up the rain and she was back issuing orders to the rest of us who were standing there, incompetent in our awe of the storm.

Here was a young woman whom I envisioned was destined for great things. However, as the days went on, she was not always in good standing with those in authority because she was often late in arriving for assignments, prayer gatherings and meals. If she saw something that called for action, she was in it without hesitation no matter what other duties might be waiting for her attention. She was the most unique young lady I had ever met; she was completely at ease. It never seemed to bother her that some looked upon her as a dizzy whirling dervish. That ease in making decisions appealed to me. Sad to say, Lorrie, with her marvelous spirit of freedom did not stay long in our company. She decided that she needed to pursue whatever the Lord sent across her path.

The rest of us went about this large complex serving in many capacities. We cleaned, served in the dining hall, helped in the hospital laundry, and aided the cooks in the hospital kitchen. We learned how to sew our own habit (a nun's dress) according to the minute specifications of the rule and of course, we prayed and studied.

As we interacted with some of the older nuns while helping in various parts of the convent and hospital, we had a chance to observe what they contributed to bettering this world, how they showed their dedication and how they responded to everyday difficulties. Among them were several that I would classify as real "characters."

One of them, Sister Loretta, was in charge of the hospital laundry. She rarely talked. Her face, placid and peaceful, rarely changed even when facing the mountains of laundry that needed washing, ironing, and distributing to many locations in the convent and in the hospital every day. She worked long hours doing her job perfectly and apparently without looking for any praise. She pushed her huge cart heaped with freshly laundered linens down the halls and into the elevators. She personally delivered them to each floor and department. "Sister Monica Rose, I want you to come with me to help unload the linens. Pay attention to any complaints the nurses might make about the linens we deliver. We are here to serve."

I was surprised to hear her speak at such length but pleased to accompany her. If there were any complaints, she wanted to hear them herself. As far as I remember, nobody every complained about her work. She patiently taught us her methods. She expected nothing but the best from us. We happily followed her unselfish example even when it was very hot and humid in her steamy workplace.

Character two, Sister Emma, was a tiny, sweet, talented seamstress who barely spoke any English. She was in charge of the large sewing room that kept hospital linens mended. She created all of the white habits that the nursing nuns wore in their healing work, as well as the black habits of the nuns who worked in the offices. She also was in charge of teaching all of us new members how to sew, mend, and make our new habits. Almost all of what we wore was made right there in her sewing room. Following her ever-patient demonstrations, we soon learned to proficiently heed her silent directions for sewing a perfect seam or producing an even hem.

Character three, Sister Rose, took charge of the huge kitchen that produced the wonderful meals served in the hospital for patients, workers, nurses and nuns. We helped here several times a week and learned how to keep food clean, properly cooked, and appetizingly prepared for serving. Many lay people helped right along side of us. Sister Rose insisted that all foods be prepared as if we were going to present them to Jesus at his next meal. She reminded us often "Whatever we do for the least of his brethren, we do unto him." We learned how to keep the kitchen spotless so that it would always pass the scrutiny of the strictest health inspectors. Sister Rose was a bit intimidating but she was always ready to forgive our failures to pass her rigid standards for food preparation as long as we learned from our mistakes.

Besides these interesting nuns, there were older nuns who took turns supervising our evening hour of "recreation." For this respite from our long hours of silence, work and prayer, we occasionally went outdoors to play softball or volleyball or we would just go for a walk. Other times, we sat around a table while we mended our stockings, did hand sewing on a new article of clothing or listened to an older nun tell stories of her life experiences.

One such nun was a very eccentric nurse, Sister Beatrix. She could tell stories that kept us enthralled for the entire hour she spent with us at least once a week. During the war when most of the doctors had been called for service elsewhere, she was in charge of monitoring the mothers who were about to give birth in the hospital. She told how the doctors would chew her out if she called them too soon or too late for the delivery. She missed the mark many times and had to deliver the babies alone! She had a way of telling her stories, amplified with comical facial expressions that kept us laughing and longing for her next turn to be with us.

From all of these nuns, I gleaned a great deal of knowledge about work ethics. Mostly, I learned these nuns didn't fulfill their jobs because they were seeking worldly praise or recognition. They did not find their worth or value in their accomplishments. They taught me that God's view about performance and acceptance came from the love of Jesus, who gave his life for each of us no matter how different we are. Each of these nuns, though of different and far from perfect personalities, lived by a clear principal: "God does not measure our worth based on human standards of acceptance." By their constant fidelity, they witnessed that, besides Jesus, nothing has any lasting significance. He alone mattered to them. Their faithfulness and good deeds came from abiding in him who strengthened them each day. I have always cherished what I learned from these wonderful nuns.

We learned to pray the daily reading of "The Office." This was a book of prayers, taken mostly from the Book of

Psalms, divided into "Hours" of the day. *Prime* was the Morning Prayer, *None,* the prayers recited at about noon, *Sext,* prayers at suppertime and *Vespers,* the evening prayers. We sometimes recited these prayers together in the chapel or we said them as we walked outside on a lovely, long, circular, shaded path called Rosary Road that lead to the community cemetery.

Little by little, the messages of those beautiful psalms began to take root in my heart. It taught me a great deal about prayer and showed me that I could experience the presence of God in any situation. These psalms revealed people rejoicing, mourning, asking forgiveness, recalling the past, and imagining the future. They taught me how to love God, how to obey him, and how to be a light to others. Repeatedly, each day, God impressed upon my mind and heart that no matter how holy or sinful we may feel, each of us is on the same pathway of discipleship. There is nothing that we can do that will ever lessen God's love for us nor is there anything we can do to ensure that he will love us any more. He loves us unconditionally and that is that! As I saw things in myself that needed to change, I learned to praise God. It meant that he was at work in me, changing me a little bit more into the person he wanted me to be. I kept praying for strength and wisdom. I tried to banish all my anxieties and fears. I always found him right at my side offering me his love and his peace. Any difficulties I faced, I believed, would contribute to my growth as a Christian and it would forge my character into a servant of the Lord.

Another welcome addition to life in this place was a weekly class taught by one of the monks from a nearby Benedictine Abbey. These priests came to teach us Scripture and Theology. Again, I would sit in those classes, usually conducted in the chapel, and try to absorb every truth they taught. They didn't stress rules and regulations but emphasized prayer, recognizing our relentless human hunger to communicate with God. They told us about the pitfalls of discouragement and doubt. Their messages contained words of consolation for us. They also seemed to have an endless supply of great jokes to share. These priests were very different from most of the parish priests that I had encountered in my youth growing up in Verona, North Dakota. These priests were truly an inspiration.

So, I made it through my second probation period, although I still had persistent doubts. The night before making my first temporary vows, I desperately tried to think of a legitimate way to avoid taking those vows. As I walked alone in an upstairs hallway, I approached a little shrine of the Virgin Mary set up on a table at the end of that hall. I knelt there to beg Mary to send me a sign that would unmistakably tell me whether I should really take up those vows, or if I should tell my mother, Bessie, and my sister, Mary, that I wanted to go back home with them. I thought that my mother might be disappointed that I had taken so long to make up my mind. She might shed a few tears but I knew, with certainty, that there would be no reproach.

I got no sign except my own misgivings, which I was too afraid to follow. I made those vows the next day, September 15, 1947 knowing full well that I was in this for another five years. I was just one month shy of being 18 years old. .

My mother, my sister, Mary, and my niece, Nikke, had come to be with me on this occasion. The Abbot of the nearby monastery came to our chapel to receive our vows. Then came a wonderful reunion meal where we visited with our families for the first time since their arrival the day before. I never told Mom about my doubts. It was so good to visit with her and Mary, and to play with my little niece, Nikke. I had made a choice, and I would stick with it for the next five years.

Very soon after that, my Superiors told me to get ready to go back to Oakgrove, North Dakota to one of the community's small rural schools to "earn" my high school diploma.

Chapter 8
Back to School

For some reason, I did not go to North Dakota until the middle of January 1948. Then I went to "finish" high school at Oakgrove, where the nuns of our order ran a Catholic School. I sat in the classroom with the other students, but the teaching nun never called upon me to answer questions or to participate in any discussions. At first, the students thought that I was some kind of supervisor because nobody introduced me to them. I just appeared one day; the students drew their own conclusions. But soon, after school hours, my superior told me to supervise the boarders at meals, study halls, and recreation periods. At first, I was very shy but soon the students accepted me and often told me that they preferred that I "police" them because I was so much younger than all the other nuns at the school.

My official school records state that I graduated not

from Oakgrove but from St. Caitlin High School in Valley Center, North Dakota on May 28, 1948. No matter what the records say, I did not share in any graduation ceremonies at either place. At the time, I found it appropriate not to actively participate in this ceremony. I didn't believe I had really earned a diploma because those in authority falsified my credits. On the night my "classmates" graduated, I sat in the choir loft watching them accept their diplomas from the parish priest. I experienced strong feelings of inadequacy because I knew that these graduates had honestly worked and deserved to be in this ceremony. I never saw my diploma if there was ever one made out in my name.

With time and through many similar experiences, I eventually learned that those feelings of weakness and vulnerability could prove to be a bonus rather than a barrier. I learned to depend on God's help instead of my own capabilities. Those experiences taught me to trust, to pray, and to thank God for the gifts that He had given me. This helped me so that I was able not just to cope but also to enjoy what I was doing in His name. The "Good News" is that God never intended us to love and serve him on our own strength. He wants to live in us by the Holy Spirit who will provide the strength and wisdom we need each day.

After my "graduation," I spent the next two weeks scrubbing and shining everything in that school to have it ready for the fall term. Many of the other Sisters went off to teach catechism in the surrounding parishes that did not have a Catholic school in their towns. Prudently, my superiors spared me from that task that first summer.

After finishing the end-of-school-year cleaning, I boarded the train for Great Falls, Montana, to start earning my teaching degree. We always traveled in the coaches, carried our own food, and avoided contact with other passengers as much as possible. By the time we reached our destination, we were quite disheveled, weary, and ready for sleep on a good bed. We stayed at a convent owned by the Ursuline nuns. They gladly shared their boarding school with us during the summer when their usual guests were enjoying a vacation from school.

Their spacious convent was located about a mile from the college where we would be taking our classes. We walked to the college twice each day because we returned to the convent for our noon meal. The morning walk was refreshing but by noon on many days, the heat beat us down. After a good meal and a short rest, we returned for our afternoon classes.

Like most first-year students, I had no idea what college entailed. When I went to register with the other nuns who had attended this college other summers, I was lost. Nobody had time to tell me which classes I should take. I was accustomed to having my superiors assign my tasks. Again, those feelings of being alone, simple-minded, and inadequate assailed me. I had to remind myself repeatedly that God promised to be with me every step of the way. That included all my missteps too. I discovered that when those feelings tended to overwhelm me, if I prayed and began trusting in God's promises, a sense of peace was my reward. With a more peaceful mind, my stress level dropped, my headaches subsided, and I became more confident, not in my own wisdom but in the help that God provides for those who ask for it. I would not only survive, I would succeed in whatever God asked me to do. I knew full well that He always equips us for the work He gives us.

The nun in charge of registration was a Sister of Providence. This order of nuns operated the whole college. She was very helpful. I informed her that I would be teaching the next year but I did not know in which of our schools that would be, nor did I know what kind of classes I would be teaching. She encouraged me to take basic classes that would help prepare me to teach in any classroom. She signed me up for General Psychology,

Teaching Social Studies, Tests & Measurements, and the Principles of Elementary Education. *Those courses were basic?* I had been hoping to take some classes such as English composition, grammar, or math courses. That was my idea of what basic meant. Nevertheless, I took her advice and enrolled in those unfamiliar courses.

I studied consistently and prayed with a trusting heart all during that summer session. I did my very best to understand every part of each class that I took. I was exhausted at the end of the six weeks, but I was not despondent. On the contrary, I was exhilarated, knowing that I aced all of the final exams and truly earned the twelve credits issued to me! My self-esteem went up a few pegs, as did my trust in the Lord to guide and help me in all my needs. If I had let myself descend to the depths of self-pity, how different the results would have been.

Chapter 9
My First Teaching Assignment

Summer was nearly over and it was almost time for school to begin. All of us who had been studying in Montana returned to Valley Center for the annual retreat. It was a week devoted to prayer and to rest. I relished both.

Except for my personal prayer experiences while away at college, ever since I had made my vows, I felt that my spiritual life was almost stagnant. Back in community where everything came under rules and regulations, I went through the motions of community prayers, but my life in the Spirit was sluggish. There was just so much going on that was at odds with my conscience. I felt that I was forever climbing an impossible hill. Community prayers were often just an arid recitation of litanies, rosaries, and prescribed readings. Prayers from the heart were difficult for me during most days. Again, the temptation to feelings of hopelessness screamed for my consent. It was hard to keep my eyes on the Lord though he was right there to help me.

All during the retreat, our Mother Provincial held private interviews with each nun to discuss what her duties would entail for the coming year. Every nursing nun, teaching nun, cook, seamstress, and those who filled other positions attended this annual retreat or another one that had been held earlier in the summer. As I waited my turn, I experienced great feelings of apprehension. I did not feel ready to face a classroom of little children who would look to me to teach them the fundamentals they needed.

On the last day of the retreat, the long awaited call came for my interview. Mother Margaret, the Provincial of our area, informed me that for the school term of 1948-49 I would be teaching in Willowton, North Dakota at Notre Dame Academy (This was just a high school but the title "Academy" made me think it was of a special quality.) I stared at her in complete dismay. I wanted to scream in protest. *What was she thinking?* I had not really finished my own high school education, and this superior was sending me to teach students that were my own age? Incredible! My mind was in a state of complete rebellion.

Then, I remembered what Mother Gertrude had taught, "You are not to question what is asked of you. Blind obedience is the rule." Here indeed, I needed to rely on God's strength. My lack of experience had nothing to do with any given assignment. I could not in good conscience say, "I can't do this! I don't want this responsibility!" I had taken the vow of obedience. I asked myself, *"Where is your commitment? Did you expect to be sitting in an easy chair for the next year?"* I did venture to ask what subjects I would be teaching. Mother calmly replied, "That will be left to the discretion of your new superior, Mother Patricia."

My heart took another great leap of apprehension. Grapevine gossip is extensive even in the convent. I had heard a few daunting tidbits about that nun. She was the first ever non-French woman in our convent system appointed as a superior. I had heard she ruled with an iron hand. I guessed she had to prove that she was just as capable a Mother Superior as were the French nuns. Oh, Mama Mia, I was not looking forward to the school year at all!

Upon my arrival at Willowton, a tiny little village in northern North Dakota, it didn't take Mother Patricia long to outline my schedule and to set off a few more alarms to shatter my already badly eroded peace of mind. She began, "You will be teaching first year typing to the sophomores."

Just after I retrieved my jaw from where it had fallen below my knees, I summed up enough courage to mention that I had never, ever touched a typewriter in my life. She replied casually, "Then you'll just have to learn in a hurry, won't you?"

She was one doughty woman. I guess I should have been grateful that she didn't expect me to teach Typing II.

"Besides typing," she went on. "You will also teach Junior Business and World Geography."

My nerves tied themselves in knots. The words "Junior Business" slammed against my heart. I had not handled so much as a penny since the day I entered the convent. *What did I know about business? Would I find time to sleep if I had to learn all of this foreign material before school started?* I didn't think it possible, but I dared not voice that doubt to her. Then she told me something that truly shocked me. She said, "Notre Dame Academy is fully accredited by the state. Since you have only a few hours of college credits, you will teach under the name of Sister Mary Cecelia, a nun now retired because of old age. When the state inspectors come here, you are to answer to that name. Do you understand?"

I wanted to scream out in protest, "Yes, I fully understand that you want me to lie to the state inspectors

69

when they come to my classroom." I was a coward. I did not want to believe my ears. My superior was asking me to lie about my teaching credentials and about the name given me to signify my new commitment to Christ. I was totally confused, worried, and just plain panic-stricken.

Without much more ado, Mother Patricia gave me the teaching manuals and told me to get busy. I studied every spare moment that I could. I was not relieved of any of my other duties, which always included cleaning and polishing everything in the school. When the boarders started arriving for the fall term, I had to find a room where they would not see nor hear me practice typing. I was so tense that I could hardly concentrate, let alone become a proficient typist. I thought that I would never learn fast enough to fool high school students. Migraine headaches continued to be my daily cross to bear.

Mother Patricia, who liked exercising her authority, was never gracious about handing out any supplies. It called for extreme need on my part before I went to her for any necessities. I always felt that I was in debt to the community for supplying me with soap, stockings, shoes and all other essentials. When I asked her if I might have a supply of aspirin, she said, "No, you need to learn how to work through the pain." She would not allow me to have a bottle of aspirins to use at my own discretion. I was miserable, at least physically, most of the time. Each morning I woke up with a pounding headache. I prayed that the Lord would see me through my hours of study, work, and prayer. If I had not him to rely on, I would never have made it through each day. I never questioned why this was happening to me. I trusted the Lord, but I was losing my respect and admiration for some of the superiors who thought they were above obeying moral laws. It was very difficult to understand why they didn't realize that with a little relief from pain my teaching efforts would have been more successful.

Classes started. I entered my first classroom shaking like a leaf in a windstorm. I tried to appear poised and in control. I distracted my typing students by letting them get their fingers on the keyboard right away. I didn't spend much time explaining the parts of a typewriter to them as the manual had advised. I needed them to be thinking about their task of learning the location of the various keys. I did not want them to focus on my shaking body or any other part of me. It worked. Soon the clatter of the machines drowned out the tumultuous thumping of my heart. The students were impressed because they were learning so fast. That meant trouble for me. I would have to stay up late each night to study the next steps to keep ahead of them! But God was watching over me. Even if others made bad decisions for me, he was always there with help if I asked. I asked!

One student was an accomplished piano player. She caught on to "touch typing" in no time at all. She led the class in speed and accuracy. She often came to my aid when questions came up that would have exposed my ignorance. She quickly raised her hand and offered the proper solution. I found more kindness in her than I saw in the woman who had responsibility over me.

Still, there was no need for me to feel crushed by weights that I felt that I could not carry. Either I would give God my burdens and cease all the strife, or I could proceed on my own strength that might last for a while where eventually I would have fallen on my face in abject failure.

To my relief, the students never asked me to demonstrate my typing speed that was indeed pitiful! They were convinced that I was a great teacher. By the end of the first semester, most of them were typing like pros.

Though I knew nothing about business, teaching Junior Business was not all that complicated. The same was true of World Geography. I was quick to learn the basic facts of both of those subjects, but I was always afraid that at any given moment the students would recognize me for the fraud that I was. They never did. Mistakenly they thought that I was some sort of a genius who had finished college at a very early age. I did not feel great about this deception.

Chapter 10

The Teacher Continues to Learn

Several of the older, male boarders took great delight in flirting with me whenever they could without Mother Patricia detecting their outrageous behavior. Her stern discipline ordinarily kept them within acceptable boundaries. They could perhaps sense that because of my youth, they could have a little fun with me. There was not a whole array of exciting activities as a legitimate outlet for these young men with their raging hormones. One senior student was especially obnoxious. One day, after he had made a very explicit pass at me, instead of just passing it off as youthful lightheartedness, I lost my temper and gave him a resounding slap across the face. Immediately, I was remorseful and terribly frightened. This student was very bright; he recognized his chance to hold me hostage. He said, "Just wait until my mother comes to pick me up this weekend. You will be one sorry nun for hitting me."

He was correct in that last assumption. I was very sorry for lashing out at him in such a violent manner but I certainly could not let him get by with his offensive behavior. I would have to deal with my own inexcusable actions later. Feigning a nonchalance that my heart certainly did not feel, I shrugged, "Go right ahead, young man. I am sure your mother will be happy to hear from Mother Patricia just how rudely you have been treating me."

My casual manner worked its startling magic. From that day on, I never had a speck of trouble from him or any of the other young men. Whew! I thanked the Lord for giving me the presence of mind to call his bluff. However, I learned from this experience that I had to curb my temper and never again resort to striking a student in anger. I needed to learn that lesson early in my teaching career. Although this student needed discipline, it was not my place to resort to violence. I knew that I had to lighten up in my reactions to all the students. I could not let the stress I was feeling in my personal life become a source of unfairness and unnecessary grimness when dealing with my students. Little by little, I learned to relax whenever I was in charge of student activity. Relying on the Lord's power and putting my trust in him helped me to see that the students were just having fun and did not always need strict supervision. They still knew they had to behave in my presence; they came to respect my discipline. It was easy to see that most students like knowing where their boundaries begin and end.

I was so glad when that first year was behind me. I looked forward to summer and another stint at classes in Great Falls. Now I had some practical experience behind me. I believed that my next courses would be more meaningful.

However, there was a new mission to complete before summer school began. Teaching catechism in one of the parishes near Willowton was my assignment. *Did I get any special training for this task?* No! I just did it to the best of my ability. I followed the pattern that I had observed when nuns had taught me catechism in Verona during my childhood. Thankfully, an older nun, who was more experienced in this kind of mission, took on much of the responsibility for planning the activities for the two-week period that we spent on this mission.

Those youngsters were eager to learn about the love of God, and I was so happy to be able to teach them. We taught for only a half day, and then we could relax by visiting some of the homes in the parish as the pastor directed. Everywhere we went we were welcomed very warmly.

After completing those two weeks, once again I boarded the train with the others who were continuing their education as I was. We stayed again with the warm-hearted Ursuline nuns.

That summer of 1949 was much like the previous summer, except I was a little more confident this time around. After six weeks of intense study, we returned to Valley Center for retreat. I would follow this kind of schedule every year, with few exceptions, until I earned my BA degree in education in August 1962. Yes, it took fourteen summers for me to earn that degree.

At the retreat, my Superior informed me that I would be going back to Willowton for another year. I was not too despondent about that because I was now a little more surefooted in my ability to cope with high school students. She also told me that I could go home on August 16th for a one-day visit. I was to be back at the convent before bedtime.

I really enjoyed that one-day vacation with my family. I never breathed a word about the difficulties of my convent life. Dad happened to be home during my visit. Because of his frequent absence from our home while I was growing up, he was something of a stranger to me. He had worked on road building projects all over the state ever since the days of the Great Depression. He was a farmer at heart, but hard times had forced him to sell his beloved farm in order to feed his large family.

Since he had been a convert to Catholicism when he married my mother, he found my new life entirely beyond his understanding. During the early afternoon of our visit, Dad invited me to ride with him and mom to a nearby town. When I asked why we were going to town, he answered, "Grace, (He could not get used to my new name), I want to buy you a ring at the jewelry store. I am proud that you are a teacher and I have never bought you any presents over the years. I can afford it now."

His thoughtfulness and unusual attentiveness touched me deeply. It broke my heart to tell him that nuns in our convent could not wear rings.

"Why in the Sam Hill not?" he asked.

Dad looked bewildered and deflated. He could not understand that kind of prohibition. When I tried to explain that nuns are to live simply without expensive jewelry even if it is a gift, he just scratched his head and walked away.

Mom consoled me. She said, "I will try to explain this to him later on. He finds your wearing apparel and your rules hard to understand. He really resents the fact that you are only allowed one day a year to visit. He asked me why you have to be back in the convent tonight. This home was good enough for you for the first years of your life, and we aren't living such a low life that we will change you drastically if you slept a night at home. I agreed with him but told him we must abide by the rules, or you will not be permitted to come home again next year."

How I wanted to tell her that I also found it unreasonable that those in authority had the right to deprive me of so many pleasures that would have contributed to my well being.

He and mom delivered me back to Valley Center on time. The next day I left for Willowton to begin the 1949-50 school year.

Chapter 11
A Wolf in Sheep's Clothing

Before school started, Mother Patricia decided to invite the nuns and the parish priest from Harwell, North Dakota to come for a picnic. When she threw a feast, it was quite elaborate. We had tables set out under the trees complete with tablecloths, real dishes, and a great variety of delicious well-prepared foods.

Before the guests arrived, she called me to her office. She said, "Father O'Neal will accompany the nuns from Harwell. I want you to give him special attention. Sometimes he is a very difficult man; he can be very unreasonable in his demands on the teachers. If he is happy, maybe he will go easy on the nuns in his parish during the coming school year."

I responded, "Shall I wash his feet?"

"You have the right idea. Pour on the ointment!"

It seemed that Mother Patricia did have a good sense of

humor after all. We went out to tend to our guests with a sense of purpose and with genuine smiles on our faces.

I made sure that Father had everything he needed. I didn't want my sisters who taught in his parish to have to put up with his bad temper. The day seemed to be a roaring success. In the evening, they left to go back to Harwell.

Several days later, as I was preparing for the new students in my classroom, Mother Patricia again called me to her office. She said that she had bad news for me. I thought someone in the family was sick or had died. She reassured me that it was nothing like that.

She had received a notice from Mother Margaret, the Provincial Superior, stating that I was to go immediately to St. Cecelia's School in Harwell. I would be replacing Sister Geraldine, an elementary teacher, whom Father O'Neal had just fired. He specifically had asked for me as a replacement. Again, I was traumatized with this unexpected change of assignments to another school, just days before the fall term began. I could not understand what was happening. I was again distressed that something like this could happen in convent life; that a pastor could fire a nun was news to me.

Mother began to clue me in on the situation that had arisen because of my attentive care of Father O'Neal at that picnic. She said that he was very impressed with me, and that Sister Geraldine was just too old to be teaching in his school. She further warned me that this priest had a reputation of wanting the attention of young nuns. Now she was really scaring me. I was not sure what she meant by those words. She told me to be ever on my guard, never to be alone with him. That was all she needed to say. I decided right then and there that I would not give him more than the time of day if I could help it. Then I began to wonder why she had chosen me to attend to the priest's needs on the day of the picnic. If he were some kind of ogre who needed a young nun's attention, she should have warned me to keep my distance. What was really going on here? Red flags went up in my mind. Was I headed for danger?

The very next day I had to pack my things and leave. I was headed to a place where someone in authority might cause me potential problems.

When I arrived, Father was right there to greet me. I nodded coldly and said not a word in response to his warm welcome. That was a mistake. He immediately saw that something had changed in my demeanor between the picnic and this day. My new superior, Mother St. John, didn't have a clue about what was taking place, or at least she didn't let on that she did. As the days passed and Father did not try to corner me anywhere, I began to relax. That was another mistake.

One day, shortly after school had started, I was herding my students back to the classroom after their afternoon recess. Suddenly Father appeared, as I was about to close the classroom door. He grabbed my arm and motioned that I follow him into the Sisters' private apartment located right next to my classroom. I held back saying, "I can't leave my students alone and unsupervised."

"This is my school and you need to do as I say. The children will be fine for a few minutes."

Reluctantly, I followed him into our private living room.

He demanded to know who had changed my opinion of him. "Was it Sister Berard? She never liked me when she was teaching here."

I assured him that Sr. Berard had not said a word to me about him. That was the absolute truth.

He angrily retorted, "You are lying! She must have said something because your attitude is entirely different now than it was when I first met you in Willowton!"

By this time, I was in tears and in a state of complete terror. I fired back, " I don't give a damn what you think!

You have no right to talk to me this way." (The naughty childhood vocabulary that I had learned from my brothers erupted with force.)

Just then, the phone began to ring. I started to move to answer, grateful for the interruption. He stopped me by yelling, "Let it ring! We are not through yet."

I told him, "I am through. I am going back to my classroom."

He blocked my way before I could escape. The phone continued to ring incessantly and I continued to tremble in the same manner. I had never before openly opposed anyone in religious authority over me.

From out of nowhere, Mother St. John appeared at the door. She had left her private piano student to answer the phone that had been ringing persistently. When she saw me in tears, she calmly answered the phone. I had never seen her so in control. After replacing the receiver and jotting something on a note pad, she demanded to know what was going on. I was crying much too hard to explain. Father began to stammer and stutter in an attempt to cover his proverbial ass. Sizing up the situation, Mother told me to go into the washroom to refresh my face and then to return to my classroom. I was only too happy to oblige.

I wondered what would happen when those two went at it. Mother was a stubborn strict French nun and Father was an obstinate unpredictable Irish priest. However, I was glad to be out of it. I never learned how Mother St. John handled the situation but from that day on, Father's hostile attitude toward me matched mine toward him. Whenever he happened to meet me alone in a hallway or on the stairs, he whispered, "You're done! No matter where you go after this school year, I'll alert the parish priest that you are a troublemaker."

I never answered him. For the remainder of that year, I just minded my own business. Mother St. John never explained what transpired between her and the priest after I had gone back to my classroom. I thought she would have had some words of advice for me, but evidently, she had concluded that I had handled myself well enough.

I always wondered if Father told her that I said, "I don't give a damn!" That kind of language surged up in me unexpectedly in that time of stress. I think now that it was quite appropriate. His threat to blackball me with other pastors was just a bluff because in all my future assignments, I never had any trouble from any parish priest where I taught -- I never again had to deal with a priest who was so ornery.

It was no big surprise that at the end of that school year, my superiors did not reassign me to teach at St. Cecelia's. I held no grudge against that priest. I had no clue as to what made him act the way he did. It was not my place to judge him. He is now long gone from this world. May he rest in peace. I learned from him to be on my guard against any potential wolf in sheep's clothing.

Book Three
A Rookie No Longer

It is written in the prophets: "They shall all be taught by God."
Everyone who listens to my Father and learns from Him comes to me.
John 5:45

Education forms the common mind. Just as the twig is bent, the tree's inclined.
Alexander Pope, Epistle to Cobham, l. 149-50

Chapter 12
Relaxing and Reevaluating

In the summer of '50, I took an easy academic load at Great Falls. I earned thirteen credits studying Curriculum Workshop, Fundamentals of Music, Art Education, and Folk Dancing.

Folk Dancing fit right into my need for some relaxation. Ordinarily, we could take one day to visit our parents each year. There was never another time for a vacation unless a retreat came under that heading. So, many nuns enjoyed taking this class as a means of staying fit and relaxing.

We were not exactly "Flying Nuns" as we learned and practiced these quaint dances borrowed from other lands. As we practiced, in an all-nun class, it must have made quite a sight as our long robes and flying veils whirled around to the beat of such square dances as "Cotton-Eyed Joe" and to lively Scottish and Polish music. This course, intended to help those who might need to teach Physical

Education, was for me just plain fun. I never envisioned having to teach Physical Education to anyone. I should have known better.

After summer school, I attended my first Catholic Teachers' Convention at Sacred Heart Academy in Fargo. After the first day's session, I called my Aunt Christine Noonan who lived in Fargo. She said, "I am so glad you called. Jim is home from teaching in Page, North Dakota. Do you have time to come for a visit while he is home?"

"My evening is free if I can find my way to your house," I replied.

"Jim will pick you up as soon as you are ready," she offered.

Jim was about six years older than I was but he was many years more mature. He was an only child, but his parents must have given him lots of responsibility as he was growing up. As we traveled the distance to his parents' home, he raised questions about what I was learning at this convention. One of his most surprising questions was, "Just what is your philosophy of teaching?"

I don't think that I answered "Dah?" but that is about how I felt. I was ignorant of the need for a philosophy of teaching. When he saw my obvious discomfort, he kindly did not pursue that topic any further, but he began to tell me about his own viewpoint. "I seek the bright side of life and the good side of people in all of my experiences and in my teaching."

"That is a very noble philosophy. I bet it is hard at times to follow it."

"So far, so good," he laughed.

"You will have to tell me about what you have been doing these past few years," I encouraged.

He replied, "Well, I graduated valedictorian from Leonard High School where sports also played a big part of my life. I was on the North Dakota American Legion All-State baseball team and I won first place in the 200 yard

86

dash state track meet."

"In other words, you were fast on your feet and brilliant in your brain," I teased. "What did you do after your graduation?" I asked with genuine interest while my inner eye suddenly saw how my impetuous leap into the convent had resulted in a stunted growth in some areas. *Now I understand what my mother tried to tell me. Normal school life is needed for natural maturing. Too late smart!*

Jim continued, "I enrolled in the Civil Engineering program at the North Dakota Agricultural College for two years before I enlisted in the Naval Reserves. I graduated from the Midshipmen's School at Notre Dame as an Ensign U.S.N.R."

"I am impressed," I complimented. "Were you assigned to any active duty?"

"Yes, I was with the Amphibious Force aboard the LST 1016 in the Philippines. Our unit was very active at the end of WWII in transporting equipment, supplies, and personnel to many locations in the Pacific, including stops in Japan, Guam, and Saipan."

"You have seen a good part of the world already, haven't you?" I ventured.

"I think my most interesting experience was when we transported 800 war prisoners to Tokyo."

"I had no idea all of this was part of your life. When did you get back to civilian life?" I asked.

"Our last trip ended in June of 1946 when the 1016 was decommissioned and so was I. I went back to college and earned my BS degree in education in 1948 and since then I have been teaching in Page, North Dakota."

With this, we arrived at our destination. Uncle Jim (Mom's youngest brother) and his wife, Aunt Christine were waiting on the front porch. They greeted me very warmly. Uncle Jim motioned to his son, Jim Jr., "Bring that rocker over here for Sister so that she can sit by me." Then he asked, "And how is your mother? Is she well?"

87

"The last I saw her she was just fine. She was a little worried about Mildred because she just married this summer and she and her husband have moved to Alaska. Millie doesn't like it there at all, because they are living in a tent. Housing if very expensive and they are just starting out."

"I can understand why Bessie would be upset about that. Millie is the youngest and your mom and dad enjoyed having her at home these last years when all the rest of your brothers and sisters had left the nest," mused Uncle Jim.

"You can bet that I wouldn't like living in a tent after being so comfortable at home," rejoined Aunt Christine.

"What about the rest of the family," asked cousin Jim. "Lil graduated the same year I did. Where is she now?"

"Lil is married and has three children, Sharon is about 6, Dennis is 4 and Paula is 2. They live in Minneapolis."

Uncle Jim asked, "What about those brothers of yours? Are they all married?"

"No, Don is the only one of the boys who has married and, so far, there are no children," I replied. "If you are wondering about Agnes, she is still living in Minneapolis with her husband and two boys. The oldest boy, Jim, is nearly 10 and Doug is close to 8. Mary is working at the courthouse in LaMoure and her husband is farming. Their only daughter, Nikke, is about 6 years old now."

We continued to visit for several hours until it was time for me to get back to the convent. Jim Jr. drove me back after a very pleasant evening. I had taken it upon myself to visit with them without asking anyone's permission. I didn't even have one guilty feeling about it at all.

Notwithstanding, the pleasure of being with family again, I went away from this visit with some feelings of inadequacy. Cousin Jim appeared to be so well prepared for his career; I was not. Then I recalled what Jesus taught through Paul's letter to the Romans. What he wrote to the Romans in 12:6 is very pertinent to every day and age:

"Since we have gifts that differ according to the grace given to us, let us exercise them..." I had no reason to feel inferior. Whatever different gifts Jim or I had, God gave them to us to use for others. I was learning, and even though I had not known that I should have a philosophical mission statement in my memory, I worked hard for the welfare of those under my care. With God's help, I would not shortchange my students.

For the 1950-51 school year, my assignment was to teach high school again, this time at Valley Center. I had entered the convent there some five years previously. Now I was back to teach subjects yet unknown to me to students similar to the ones that I had been isolated from back then.

My next surprise came when I learned that my new Superior was none other than Mother Patricia. She had transferred to Valley Center from Willowton.

When I met with her, she told me, "This year, you will have an easy load with just three classes to teach, algebra, world geography, and typing."

Of course, I didn't bother to tell her that I had never cracked a book in any algebra course. I knew that her response would have been the usual, "You will have to learn quickly!"

"In your spare time, you will assist Sister Albertine in teaching private lessons to her many piano students." Sister Albertine was my old music teacher from my postulant days.

"Sister Albertine will assign some of her youngest piano students to you for lessons," Mother Patricia continued. *Will wonders never cease?*

I had very little natural talent for music. In the days before school began, Sister Albertine was kind enough to give me some hints about how to teach little ones so that they would find their lessons enjoyable. "You don't have a lot of talent but I can see that you will make up for it in determination," she encouraged. She was the first nun who really understood the difficulties that I faced because of my inadequate education in so many areas.

I grabbed the teacher's manuals and began to learn what I needed to know in algebra. I wanted to be a good teacher but again I was totally flabbergasted at my Superiors' lack of concern that I might be shortchanging my students. They placed a great deal of responsibility on my shoulders. Perhaps, I should have taken this as a great compliment.

Sometimes I got very discouraged when I realized that most of my Superiors cared little that I had terrible headaches each day and that I was constantly nervous, tense, and exhausted. Deep down, I was angry because the only thing that they seemed to care about was staffing their schools. The health of the teachers did not seem a major priority. However, I knew that I was responsible for my own actions, not theirs. This convent discipline did help me to go from selfishness to a life of service. I knew that if I let a spirit of discontent rule my life, I would be a sour, lifeless person without any hope of reaching out to others and my days of service would be worthless. I would serve with love and joy.

Trying to master algebra was the worst of my worries. Math had never come easily for me in grade school. Each day, I approached the class with the hope that some clever student would not have jumped a few pages ahead to ask me a question that left me with no answers.

I often scolded God for asking more of me than I could give. In my heart, I always heard him say, "My grace is sufficient for you." Each day I placed myself in his hands. Wiped out, after I finished that algebra class, I prayed for strength to carry on. My heavy woolen habit was soaked from my armpits to my waist with nervous perspiration. Of course, I had no access to deodorants in those days. I never saw the students holding their noses when I passed by, but I was always conscious of the possibility. Without time to go freshen up, I propelled myself to my next class.

As the year progressed, I vacillated often about my calling by God to this kind of life. I found that I really loved teaching and that I was good at it. I wanted to serve him to the best of my ability but I disagreed with some of what went on in the convent. Most of the nuns I lived with were so dedicated, devout and selfless. Just a few of my superiors' heavy-handed methods of governing left me wondering what their priorities were.

The year passed successfully and I lived through it, learning as much or more than my students did. My superior needed someone to accompany another nun who needed to attend St. Teresa College in Winona, Minnesota. Sister Mary Margaret was a nurse and she needed some credits to finish her nursing degree.

Arriving in Winona gave me my first taste of Minnesota. That summer of '51 was scorching hot. Winona is located in somewhat of a small valley. The hot air was humid beyond belief. Both the heat and humidity pressed down on that valley with no escape from the pressure cooker that developed. Coming from the dry heat of North Dakota, I didn't know how to cope. At least there and in Montana, the mornings and evenings were always cool. I kept drinking huge amounts water and orange juice in an attempt to beat the heat. I collapsed and my companion rushed me to the hospital. The doctor used a nautical term to describe my condition: "waterlogged." I had never heard of that condition. I just knew that I was miserable. I basked in the air-conditioned room the hospital provided until I was ready to face the outside world again.

After the first few days, I became more acclimated and I began to enjoy my classes in these new surroundings. The Franciscan Sisters ran the college and they were most hospitable. My class in the history of modern Europe was especially enjoyable. The teacher kept every class fresh and interesting. I also enjoyed taking a course in General Ethics and Psychology of Mental Health: new areas of knowledge that really intrigued me. Sister Mary Margaret was a delightful companion so the summer passed all too quickly and we soon had to return to Valley Center.

My two brothers, Gene and Fritz, had just bought a beautiful new Oldsmobile. They came to Valley to pick me up for my day at home. Gene said, "We bought this beauty to celebrate our birthdays. Fritz just turned 24 and I will be 26 in a couple of months."

"Yes, I know that. You rascals forget that you always held it over me that you were older and wiser than me," I rejoined.

Fritz said, "You are still just a kid and we are still much wiser. How old are you anyway?"

"You know that I am right behind you by only two years come October," I laughed.

"Well, hop in, Mom is trusting us to get you home safely," ordered Gene.

They delighted in showing me some of the latest gadgets on their new toy. As we were driving along Highway 1 toward Verona, all the windows in the car suddenly opened. I nearly jumped out of my skin. I yelled and grabbed my veil so it would not sail out the window. Delighted that they could still scare me, they showed me how they could control every window with the synchronized touch of four power buttons on the driver's side. This was a brand new feature available in some cars at that time.

With the windows wide open, Gene put "the pedal to the metal" and we streaked down the highway at top speed. That adventuresome ride home brought back many memories of the days when these two brothers loved to play tricks on me, tease me, and when needed, protect me.

When we arrived home, I could hardly wait to see my mom and dad and there was a great surprise waiting for me. Don and his wife, Kitty, were visiting also. Don was so proud to present to me their first-born son, Jerome, whom they had welcomed into the family in December of last year. We spent the day sharing food, experiences, and ogling over Jerome's valiant attempts to walk.

After a wonderful day with my family, the boys escorted me back to Valley Center for my annual retreat where I learned that I would be teaching high school there again with no new classes to prepare.

As the ending of that school term neared in May of '52, the time for me to take my perpetual vows loomed in my mind. According to what my superiors taught, once you made those vows, you could not, under any circumstances, get out of them. It was time for me to make up my mind. I decided that it was time tell Mother Provincial that I would not take perpetual vows when my temporary vows expired. I had no idea how I would tell my mother and family, or what I would be doing after I left. I was sure that I had to leave.

Chapter 13
Gullible and Gutless

When I approached Mother Provincial with my decision to leave the convent, she shushed me to silence. She reminded me that everyone has doubts from time to time. I wanted to tell her about all the things that had upset and appalled me during the past five years. She would not listen. She told me that *when* I made my vows in the coming summer, I would be going to France. She elaborated on that by saying she wanted me to see and experience where this community of nuns had its beginning. She assured me that a summer away from college studies would do me a world of good, that I would come back from a wonderful trip to France, refreshed and renewed in spirit.

When faced with moral dilemmas, I had never learned how to stand up to an authority that claimed they were "God's Voice." I battled with long-standing teachings that praised the Saints of the Church who practiced "blind obedience." Superiors held them up as models for me to imitate to the limit. Was I really supposed to leave all decisions up to those in authority? I didn't know where to turn for advice.

I began to doubt my own ability to discern the will of God. Besides those factors, a chance to travel to a foreign country really intrigued me. As the days passed, I continued to struggle through my classes, music lessons, community living, and with my conflicting thoughts about taking vows for life. On one such day, Mother Provincial told me that Father Devor, our chaplain, was waiting in the recreation hall to take my photo for the passport that I would need for entering France. A trip to France was very much a "fait accompli" as far as I could tell. I thought I might know what Jesus had felt when he was dying on the cross as he said: "It is finished." I believed that the decision was out of my hands. I was spineless. I gave up, tied for life. I decided then and there that I would be the best nun that I possibly could be. From that day on, I never allowed myself to look back nor to look for excuses to "jump the traces." This would be the way that I would spend the rest of my life. Freely, with my whole heart, I gave myself to the Lord to use me as he saw fit.

At the end of that school year of 1951-'52, I prepared to leave for France. The first lap of the journey was taken by train to Autumn Vale, Illinois then on by car to Chicago where Sister Francine, Mother Mary Edwin, and I boarded the Air France line that took us through many stops from New York, Montreal, Gander, Newfoundland, and finally to Paris. (Margie had left the convent earlier because of health problems. She returned later when her health improved.)

Though it was now several years after the end of World War II, we could still see the ravages that that war had left on the landscape and on the lives of the people we met. We stayed several days in Paris where our community had several orphanages for children left destitute and alone after the war. Their plight moved me deeply, especially when they started chattering French like little magpies. They loved to have their pictures taken and Mother Mary Edwin let me take many shots of them playing and giggling for the camera.

We did not visit any museums, any famous historical sites, and certainly no hot nightspots. We might have seen the Arc de Triomphe and the Eiffel Tower from the window of the taxi we took from the airport if the taxi driver wasn't so intent on giving us Americans such an electrifying exhibition of his driving skills. We had all we could do to hang on and to keep from screaming in terror as we dodged around cars, trucks, bikes and other vehicles. Later on, we enjoyed walking around Paris. The street vendors, the sidewalk book stores, and the art displays were unequal to anything I have ever seen. So also were the couples who openly exchanged passionate kisses and embraces on the streets of that luminous city.

Another inimitable sight was the restrooms located on boulevards on many streets. They were round houses that admitted both men and women. You could see the feet of each user because there was an open space from about mid-calf length to the ground in each of the cubicles. One did not sit down to answer the call of nature. You stood with feet apart and just let it flow to the receptacle in the ground. We always carried our own supply of toilet paper in our pockets. No such supplies were in public toilets or in the convent restrooms. They simply were too poor to provide this luxury. This was one example of the level of poverty that I saw everywhere. I noted it also in the area of food, or I should say in the lack of the abundance and variety of foods that we enjoyed in America.

After visiting several other convents in Paris, where we were always given a generous share of their meager meals, we left to go by train to the Mother House in Broones, a small city in northern France.

The train ride was interesting as people surrounded us, speaking French at speeds that would defy that of our best auctioneers. That is exactly what their chattering sounded like to me. I could catch a word here and there, but for the most part, I didn't have a clue about what they were saying. Those that were traveling long distances had taken with them large loaves of bread, cheese, and bottles of wine or cider to fend off their hunger and thirst. The train moved along very quickly compared to the ones I had taken each summer to Montana. In the matter of cleanliness, the tiny restrooms were revolting.

At the Broones station, a quaint little old Frenchman met us and ushered us to his battered car. He loaded our luggage aboard while he chattered persistently; his face lit up with a toothless grin. Since we could not understand most of what he was saying, Mother Mary Edwin translated when she had the opportunity. The gist of his monologue was about his love of America and Americans because they had liberated France from the Nazis. Americans would always be welcome here he told us.

On our arrival at the Mother House, a whole delegation of nuns waited to greet us. There were many, many nuns there for the summer retreat. They had come from Belgium, Flanders, England, the Islands of Jersey, Guernsey, and many other places in France. Naturally, they all spoke French fluently except for Sister Francine and me. I was already lonesome for the good old US of A.

Chapter 14

Parlez-Vous Francais? . . .
Mais, Oui.

The other young nuns that would make up our group making perpetual vows seemed happy to meet us. They giggled outright at our timid attempts to speak French. They said they loved our accents and we, in turn, told them we loved their accents whenever they tried to speak English. They often did, as they were eager to improve the English they had been required to learn in their schools. They were as curious about us as we were of them.

The Mother House was large and well kept despite the ravages of the war that had ended in 1945. The Germans had taken over the house as an official headquarters during the war. They sent to a concentration camp in Vittel, Germany several young American nuns who had come to the Mother House to take their Novitiate training prior to

99

the war. We were relieved to learn the Germans had treated them kindly. They were not confined behind barbed wires but instead the Germans housed them and some 3,000 other foreign nationals in several resort hotels that they had commandeered as an international internment camp. Their captors allowed them to meet with others for prayer and study. These nuns spent their time reading the few books they had and in being of service to other prisoners who needed encouragement and help.

I don't remember much about where I slept, what I ate or where I received the daily lessons that prepared us to make our final vows. I do remember the chapel that was not anything out of the ordinary except for some very unexpected dwellers that landed no matter where I knelt. Those little critters were tiny little fleas that hopped around and landed on every praying body that came to worship.

When I asked about this annoying phenomenon, someone told me the little old men and women who came from the rest home located in a section of the convent carried the fleas. I wondered why their quarters were not cleaned or fumigated until those little buggers were dead. I had not gone through a war like they had, so I kept my mouth shut. However, I did not make peace with the fleas nor did they with me.

In the matter of personal cleanliness, perhaps because of the scarcity of water, the house rules allowed one bath a week. The sister in charge of the bathroom told us that when it was our turn to bathe, we were to don a long bathing robe in a such a manner that at no time any bare skin would show. Each person was alone so I wondered why such precautions for modesty were necessary. Much later I learned that the Jansenistic heresy that taught that the body was evil still had widespread influence in France where that heresy had its beginning. Those beliefs hung on and were evident in other ways. Our habits reflected that disapproval of the human body. When not in use, hands were to be hidden in our long sleeves. Coming back from communion, we lowered our veils over our eyes to keep ourselves separated from others.

Another incident happened that showed how the culture there was so much different from current practices back in the States. One of the older nuns died. Nuns appointed for this task, lovingly arranged her body on a board for viewing for only a day. Then the nuns placed the body in a rough wooden casket and took it to the chapel where it rested in the aisle before the sanctuary. The nuns placed wood shavings on the floor below the coffin. The purpose of this puzzled me until sometime during the service, I noticed fluid dripping from that body box. Then I realized there was no practice of embalming here in France. As a result, quick burials were necessary.

Sister Francine and I often walked around their spacious grounds while saying our rosary or praying the Office. When we finished, we moaned and groaned about our hunger pangs. We were not used to their meager meals. If we happened to pass by an apple tree with a bough weighed down too heavily with fruit, we kindly relieved it by stealing a couple of apples. These we stashed away in the deep pockets of our habits. Later when no one was around, we devoured them without any qualms of conscience. We did love the marvelous bread served without any spread each morning along with chicory flavored coffee, but the servings were very small.

On an occasional feast day, Mother Superior passed around a tin of tiny candies during our recreation period. We noted in wonderment that each nun took only one piece. They would smile and exclaim about what a treat that was. Sister Francine and I later laughed and wondered what those nuns would think if they could see Americans devour a whole Snickers bar at one time. This was definitely a change from our usual way of life.

Often we helped weed their huge garden. I remember

the extremely large beans that we picked from tall trellises where the vines grew. One day we helped bring in the hay from the fields. I really think the local nuns thought we Americans would be quite useless, but Sister Francine, who had been raised on a farm, left them far behind as she piled the hay high on the waiting wagons. I didn't do so badly either but Francine was the heroine of that warm day. An ample supply of cider was on hand to relieve our thirst. It was quite potent and before long, the whole group was laughing, singing and having a jolly time as we loaded stack after stack on the wagons. I was glad those French nuns had to readjust their opinion of us. We were not the wimps they had thought we were.

However, when it came to walking, we found we could not compete with them. Provincial Superior invited Francine and me to accompany her as she made the rounds visiting several convents in the area. She thought it would be a great opportunity for us to see the countryside and to see what their convents were like. We walked from convent to convent. At each one, our hosts served a very small snack along with several tiny glasses of wine or cider. This was definitely different from any customs I had seen in our American convents. They told us that wine and cider were available and used at all meals because pure water was very hard to obtain in most communities. I liked this custom because I liked wine. At home, my Dad always bought a bottle of wine for big holidays. I was glad to see that this simple pleasure of God's good gift was not forbidden.

When we finally had visited the last convent, we started home. By this time, both Sister Francine and I were a little tipsy because we were not used to drinking wine and cider and then walking in the heat of the day. We kept asking how far we still had to go and Mother Superior would answer with a smile, "It's just around a couple more bends in the road."

Maybe we misunderstood her broken English; it took

hours for us to get back to the Mother House. We both had blisters on our heels by that time. She never asked us on such an expedition again and I was not disappointed.

Soon it was retreat time and the concluding preparations for taking our final vows. I learned that on my return to the States, I would teach third, fourth, and fifth grades in Oakes, North Dakota. This little town was only 16 miles from my parents' farm. True to the promise I had made to myself that I would never again question my vocation, I took those vows willingly and I gave myself wholeheartedly to the Lord on September 25, 1952.

On the return trip home, we took a different route. Our plane left in the late evening from Paris. About midnight, we woke up to find that we had landed on the shore of an island. I peered out the window to see our plane surrounded by soldiers standing with guns at the ready. After several futile attempts to find out where we were, we disembarked with quaking hearts. In the beautiful airport, I saw a map that showed that we had arrived on the Island of Sao Miguel, the main island of the nine islands of the Portuguese archipelago in the Atlantic Ocean. This island is a normal Sunday evening stop when traveling from Paris to New York City. Mother Edwin had handled our tickets, so we had not been aware of this stop. We stayed there for about an hour. I wanted to walk outside to see the beauty of the seashore that was not far from the airport, but the soldiers would not allow us to leave the building until we were called to board the plane again. I never did find out why there was so much security. It was a beautiful stop before I returned to take up my duties in Oakes.

Chapter 15

Restricted and Rewarded

Even though the little town of Oakes, was not far from where I grew up, I knew very little about it. During my childhood, I had been to Oakes a few times to see the dentist. Other than that, I knew nothing about the school, the church, the pastor or the people.

I thought that I might be allowed to see my parents more often. That was not to be. The rules still permitted only one day a year to visit family. I missed them so much. My mother had always been very close to me. Now, I wondered just how painful it was for her as she passed the school when she came to Oakes for doctor appointments or other needs. She had such a loving heart, I am sure it was very difficult for her not to stop for even the briefest visit on those rare occasions.

There was a time when my brother, still not married, chauffeured my mom to Oakes on a day when my class was outside playing ball. With so many youngsters in my class, we had the makings of a great softball team. Ordinarily, at least at the beginning of the year, both teams wanted me to be their impartial pitcher. I loved playing outdoors with them and recess was as much my favorite time of the day as it was for my students.

As my brother, Gene, passed the school, he saw me out there just pitching away. (My brothers had taught me a great deal about pitching and catching while I was at home.) On that day, with a great screeching of brakes and squealing of tires, he stopped the car by the playground, rolled down the windows and yelled, "Way to go, Sister!" Then he sang out in his deep bass voice, "One, two, three strikes you're out at the old ball game!"

The students laughed and asked, "Who is that strange fellow?"

"He is just one of my brothers and the lady with him is my mother," I replied, pleased that I could get a glimpse of my mom as she tried to silence Gene in his clowning off.

After my mom and Gene continued on their way, the children were full of questions about my family. They responded exactly like I had long ago when I had seen my first nun. Mistakenly, I had thought they came from heaven and I had never associated them with a real family. I could see a kind of a dazed look come over many of my students' faces. I became more real to them on that day. I loved my brother for opening their minds to reality. Now they knew that I had come from a family just like they did.

Teaching three grades in one classroom was a new experience for me. I had about 40 students that year. Added to this, I found it very difficult to adjust my teaching methods from the high school level to grade school level. The classroom was almost too small to accommodate that number of children. I had to walk down the aisles sideways because the desks were very close to each other. I never had a problem with discipline. For the most part, the children and I got along just fine.

In this day and age, teachers and perhaps parents might rail against that number of students and classes being held in one room. It did have its drawbacks but there were some very positive factors to consider.

The older students helped the younger ones. The younger ones listened to the lessons the older students were learning. Many of them forged ahead of their grade level because of this. There was also a wonderful family feeling among all the students. They looked out for one another. If someone fell on the playground, everyone rushed to see that they were not hurt. They learned to comfort and support their classmates. If one student or another was inept as a batter, catcher, or base player, the children constantly encouraged them by showing them how to hold the bat, how to follow through with a good pitch or how to keep their eyes on the ball when catching. Even if they were put out after finally connecting the bat to the ball, they cheered them on for their good effort. It was so rewarding to see how these young people were being transformed daily, through the mercies of God, to better reflections of Jesus.

There were just two other nuns teaching with me. Sister Louisa taught the primary grades. Sister Geraldine was our mother superior and taught the two upper grades. She was a great person but a compulsive worker. She had always wanted to be a nurse yet superiors placed her in teaching. She did not seem to be cut out for teaching, in my opinion. She assigned unrealistic work and then gave outrageous new written assignments or lengthy memorization of facts as punishment when students did not hand in their homework. Her students were always complaining to me, hoping that I could intercede for them.

After the regular school day, to avoid grading the assignments that the students had handed in, she buried herself in manual labor. She constantly dusted, scrubbed, washed and ironed altar linens, polished windows and

107

waxed floors whether they needed it or not. She suffered even more than I did from migraine headaches. After exhausting herself and us with her constant need to be cleaning, she went to her bed whenever possible. It was easy to see that her life was one of frustration. Despite all this, I found her to be most likeable, as did most people, at least when she did not have headaches.

Sister Louisa was one of the nuns who had gone through the experience of that German concentration camp during WWII. She spoke rarely of her experiences as she cheerfully went about her duties. She was very prayerful, dedicated and upbeat in her outlook on life. On our walks to the hospital chapel where we attended Mass several days each week, I noticed that her walk indicated that she suffered much from arthritis. She never uttered any words of complaint about this or any other hardship in her life. If fact, she never communicated anything of her personal likes or dislikes. She just lived her life quietly in the service of the Lord.

Father McDonald was our pastor, a very good man. He prepared the worship liturgy and his sermons with great care. He was years ahead of reforms that came much later from Vatican II. He was the first priest who ever treated me like an adult. I remember the day when he asked what I thought about purchasing an electric water fountain for the children. I was dumbfounded. Nobody in the eight years that I had been in the convent had ever asked my opinion on anything. I didn't know how to respond but we did get a new water fountain.

Mother Provincial had told Father that I was an accomplished musician. He asked me to start a children's choir and an adult choir. So, that is what I did. I worked and worked with the children and the adults until the choirs preformed well.

Finally, I had developed one philosophical principal of teaching, at least in music. I always told the children,

"Anyone who can speak can sing." (Somehow or other, they never knew that I had no natural talent for singing myself.) I taught them how to listen closely to the pitch and try to match it exactly. They believed everything I told them and within a very short time, I had a children's choir that was the talk of the town.

Tackling an adult choir was much more difficult. I didn't know the difference between tenor, bass and alto, but I was able to bluff my way through that as well with the help of the able organist, Maggie Fila. She must have noticed my lack of musical skills because she made helpful suggestions and she took pains to make me look good. At that time Mass was still in Latin and we had to learn many hymns in Latin to follow the complex liturgies that Father always prepared. Maggie was so talented in her musical abilities that she covered well for me. She accomplished this with such nonchalance and such good humor that the choir members didn't seem to notice any lack of talent on my part.

One day Maggie had to leave town. There was no other organist available. Father approached me and said, "Sister Monica, here is your chance to play the organ on Sunday. I have been waiting to hear how you display the great ability that your superiors told me you possess."

I didn't say a word. Fright paralyzed me at the thought of having to play the organ. I told Mother Geraldine about it and she said, "Go to the church and practice."

I practiced and practiced but I knew that even if I had a year to prepare I would never be ready. When Sunday morning arrived, my head and heart pounded. My nerves, twisted and tortured, were at a breaking point. The children's choir sang the first Mass of the day. As they gathered in the choir loft, the pressure increased. It was time to start the first hymn. I got the first few notes played and then I froze. The children kept on singing and I was on the verge of fainting. They thought I was very sick and they carried on without my directions and did a beautiful job of singing *a cappella*. I was mighty proud of them and very disgusted with myself.

Before the second Mass started, Father asked me what had happened. I broke down and told him that I was no talented musician and that I was in fact a fraud. He was outraged, not at me, but at my superiors for lying to him. He said, "Why in the world didn't you just tell me you couldn't play the organ? I never wanted to put you through a trial like this for any reason! You go rest and we will handle the singing for this second Mass."

He then encouraged me to always stand up for my rights. It was the first time I felt validation about my misgivings about some of my superiors' underhanded ways. He agreed with me that the end never justifies the means. From that day on, I began to feel that all of my thinking had not been wrong. I was so thankful to this priest who was so different from a few others I had encountered in my life. He praised me for the work that I had been able to accomplish with the choirs and assured me that he would never again ask me to play the organ. I could have shouted for joy to the highest heaven!

That afternoon Father called at the convent to invite us to go for a ride in the country. He had a very nice car so we were very happy to put down our lesson plans to go for an unexpected outing. He drove around Oakes for a few minutes and then headed down Highway 1. He stopped in Verona at the parish house and we visited for a few minutes with the priest there. Thinking that our tour was nearly over, we looked at one another in surprise when Father turned toward the direction of LaMoure. I kept thinking how nice it would be if we could stop for just a few minutes at my parents' home which was just one mile down the road. Without asking for anyone's permission, Father turned abruptly as he neared the road to my parents' house. When the house came into view, Father said, "Sister

Monica, I need to see if your mother has any sweets on hand. I am hungry. Do you think she might put on a pot of coffee for us?"

I didn't know what to say because this was certainly out of order. When we arrived, the other sisters began to get out of the car so I knew that it would be okay. It was all Father's doing. As we came into the house, mom threw her arms around me and nearly squeezed me to death. She and dad were very happy to see us and, of course, mom had cookies and it didn't take her long to brew up a pot of coffee. Dad came up with lines he loved to say whenever they got visitors: "Now, at last, I am going to get something good to eat!"

I sat as close to my mother as I could possibly get. She kept reaching out to touch me as she entertained and served her guests. Occasionally, I noticed a tear rolling down her cheek. Soon, a matching one slid its way down my cheek. Both of us have the tendency to tear up when we are happy. We had a very pleasant visit and again I knew that I had found a true friend in Father McDonald. He so clearly understood the gentle message of love that Christ wished to be evident in all his followers.

Chapter 16
Lonesome and Lonely

Notwithstanding the many good things that happened, the year was long and difficult. Most evenings, the other two nuns, being somewhat more elderly, retired early. I was alone and lonely. One Saturday night, after an especially hectic day of scrubbing floors, washing and ironing altar linens, and preparing the church for Sunday Mass, (At this time the lay people were not asked to help with any of these tasks) I was fed up with everything. I longed for some kind of outlet for my emotions other than work, work, work.

TV was beginning to be affordable in some homes at this time. Father had bought one and on several occasions had invited us over to his house to watch the popular Bishop Sheen program. (Definitely no relation to Charlie, of "Two and a Half Men.") On this particular Saturday, I decided to walk over to the parish house and to ask if I could watch TV with Father and his housekeeper.

Father's eyes opened wide when he saw me at the door. I asked, "Are you watching TV tonight?"

With no judgment in his eyes he replied, "Indeed, I am, please come in."

He indicated a nice easy chair for me and I sat there without saying another word. He and the housekeeper looked at me out of the corner of their eyes perhaps wondering what was going on with me. At a commercial break, the housekeeper got up to make some popcorn. *O My! That is a wonderful aroma drifting in from the kitchen! Do I dare eat if they offer to share? Will I be able to resist?*

After Father's gentle urging, I indulged in this treat that had not tickled my taste buds since I had left home. I did it without a further thought of guilt. After an hour or so, I decided that I better get back to the convent before I was missed. I thanked my surprised hosts for an enjoyable evening and left. Then strong feelings of guilt arose for what I had done. It was rude of me to just appear at the rectory without explanation to intrude on their evening. I never did it again and no one ever asked me about my one-time rebellion against the austerity and isolation of my life.

Like most people, I had that same tendency to think that when things are going good, God is with me. When things are going bad, God disappears. I realized that I was allowing my negative circumstances to prevent me from hearing from God. I was more than a little disappointed with him. He was not to blame. I realized that my attitudes were pulling me down.

Prayer was always the way through my troubles. I devoted myself again to seeking God's wisdom, knowledge and values. I had seen prayer as remedy in my mother's many trials. Why had I let that lesson slip away so easily? I had seen this desert on the horizon—it had not just suddenly appeared. Now it surrounded me and as intimidating as it might be, I knew there was an end somewhere. I felt quite hopeless, yet I knew that God would help me find my way out of this dry and lonely state of mind. I knew that he does not allow us to venture into the desert to destroy us; rather, he lets us go there so he can strengthen us. I knew that it would not be the last desert that I would trudge through, and the lessons I learned here would strengthen me to follow him wherever he chose to lead me. I would stay here, learn from my experiences and be better able to encourage others through their tough times.

I recalled a story from Genesis where Joseph stands out as a character who went through one desert experience after another, beginning with an encounter in a literal desert with slave traders. Each situation Joseph endured seemed more unmerited than the last. At some point, things had to change. Joseph went from a pampered son to jail cell dweller; Joseph's life seemed to take a turn for the worse repeatedly. Yet, Joseph never doubted God. He never became bitter. Each time Joseph's circumstances deteriorated, we see how God went with him. Joseph spent many days in the bottom of a pit, but God did honor him for his faithfulness. I again determined that I would learn the lessons that God wanted to teach me here in this desert of my loneliness.

I was not very well rooted in my Christian life. I still had miles to go, many lessons to learn, many obstacles to overcome in my openness to the wisdom of the Holy Spirit. Why was God so slow in transforming my mind so that I would see the wisdom of his ways?

In Psalm 1:3, the word of God tells us that we are to be: "like a tree planted near streams of water, that yields its fruit in season; its leaves never wither; whatever they do prospers."

I needed to plant myself by the river of God's grace to become firmly rooted in his life by letting him influence every dimension of my life. I knew that he loves every person with an everlasting love and that he will always

115

remain faithful to us, even if we can't understand his overall plan. The powerful rivers of his grace will rush in and erode all the old ways of thinking and living. It will allow him to point out areas where we are not choosing him and then he will provide the help needed to make the necessary changes.

In reality, I felt more like the chaff that the next verse of Psalm 1 goes on to describe. I felt blown about without roots. Try as I might, I could not always understand what our good God was trying to accomplish in my life. *Patience!* In his way, in his good timing, he would teach me. My mother was again the beacon that showed me the right way to face difficulties.

I made my yearly day visit with my parents. This visit was always so important to me because it gave me an opportunity to catch up on the events of the family. Gene was planning to marry to a young lady from Lisbon. I learned that my youngest sister, Mildred, who had married and was living in Alaska, was pregnant again with her third child.

The last time I had visited with her was in November of 1951. She and her first-born son, Timothy, had come to visit me in the convent at Valley Center. Tim had just had his first birthday and she was very pregnant with her second child at that time. My mother told me that Millie would be coming back home to have her third baby; Robert Arthur was born on October 1, 1953 at LaMoure, North Dakota.

Shortly after that event, my sister Mary came to the door of my classroom in the middle of a school day. She beckoned me to come out in the hall so she could talk freely. I asked the children to stay quietly in their desks until I came back. I knew from the worried, sad look on my sister's face that there was bad news. With tears in her eyes and voice, she related what had happened.

Shortly after Bobby was born, Mildred and her

husband, Roger, were traveling back to Alaska. Their life in Alaska was tough and Mildred had not wanted to go back there. Since that was where her husband was making a living, she agreed reluctantly to go with him. Somewhere in Montana, Mildred had her first nervous breakdown. Roger called my mother to ask what he should do. Mother asked my brother-in-law, Harold Gleesing to go with my brother, Paul, to bring Mildred back home. Some of Roger's relatives in Montana kept the children.

Mary begged me to come home to comfort my mother as she prayerfully waited for Mildred and the men to arrive. Surprisingly, my superior, Mother Geraldine, quickly gave her permission. She didn't even call Valley Center to see if it was all right. She got a substitute for my classroom and I went home with Mary.

There we prayed and wept together as we waited for the arrival of Mildred, Harold and Paul. We clung to the Lord, knowing that we were powerless to change events but hopeful that he would help us bring Mildred back to health.

When Mildred came through the front door supported by my brother, I took one look at this very disheveled woman who did not really resemble my baby sister at all. Her eyes were blank, her face showed no recognition of where she was. Stunned, I turned and went out the back door sobbing my heart out. I couldn't believe that my sister had been going through such horrific trials that she had attempted to take her own life while she was traveling back to Alaska. She was completely depressed and she could not get out of that depression by herself.

Instead of being a comfort to my mother, my mother had to comfort me. While doing that, she settled Mildred down at the dining room table and tried to get her to eat but Mildred was far beyond the point where she would eat. Dad and Mom decided that they would take her to the hospital in Oakes. I rode along with them to the hospital.

I tried to compose myself so that Mildred would not see

how distressed I was. She was too far out of it to take any notice of me. At the hospital, the doctor gave her some kind shot to quiet her. As she became more restful, we began to talk. She had many confusing ideas circulating around in her head. She talked of a musician, Whoopee John in one sentence and about her baby boys in the next. She continued to ask about her children and who was caring for them. Finally, she fell asleep. Dad could not understand what was happening to his little girl. He didn't know where to turn for answers. Mom was the strong one comforting him and me, never thinking of her own sorrows at all.

I returned very late to my protected life in the convent. Sleep would not come. I could feel all the anguish of the day. This was my first experience with mental illness and it struck with horrifying strength since it concerned my sister whom I so dearly loved. My problems diminished in intensity as I compared them to what Mildred was going through. I prayed through the rest of the night.

Chapter 17
Why do Bad Things Happen?

The next day, my mother called to ask if I could accompany her and Gene to the Twin Cities where they had found a hospital and a doctor to treat Mildred's condition. I received permission to do that, but with it came strict instruction that I had to find a convent in the Cities to spend the night if I had to be gone for more than one day. My mother reassured my superiors that they would follow their orders to the letter.

The trip was uneventful until we stopped for food some place in Minnesota. Gene parked at a fast food place that was very close to a lake. He went in for some carryout food. He left the keys in the ignition. As we sat there with Mildred in the front seat and Mom and me in the back, Mildred kept eyeing the keys. Mom told me to go up in front to sit with Mildred. Mildred laughed and said, "Mom, don't worry, I am not going to drive us into the lake." It was the first time we heard her laugh since she had come home the previous day.

After eating our lunch in the car, we continued with our journey until we arrived at the hospital in Golden Valley. When Mildred saw the building, she realized that we were going to leave her there. She did not want to get out of the car. The attendants came and forced her to get out. We watched helplessly with intense feelings of sadness as she struggled to get away from them. Finally, they had to subdue her with a tranquilizer. Sobbing quietly, she relaxed and they carried her into the hospital.

We stayed with her until she fell asleep. It was late afternoon. My mother and Gene intended to stay overnight at my sister Aggie's home so that they might talk to the doctors the next day. Though worn out by the emotional stress, Mom meant to keep her promise to my superiors. "We have to find a convent for you before it gets any later."

I longed to stay with her at my sister's home. Aggie was my oldest sister. I had spent a summer with Aggie when her two boys were very young. Now Jim was almost twelve years old and Doug was getting close to his tenth birthday. Mom knew I had to abide by the rules, so she said, "Gene, find a phone book -- call some Catholic parishes until you find a convent where your sister can sleep tonight."

Mom, though thoroughly exhausted, saw that I was hurting. My head was pounding. I had not slept at all the previous night. Mom pulled out a bottle of aspirins from her purse and told me to take it with me. I popped two of them in my mouth immediately and returned the bottle to her. I didn't feel right in taking pills because my superiors usually frowned on this practice. Meanwhile, Gene found a phone book and after several calls to Catholic rectories, he found a convent that would take me in. They dropped me off there and left with the promise to pick me up the next morning before returning to the hospital.

The next day we visited Mildred again. She was not very happy with us. This was very understandable. She was ill with postpartum depression. She was feeling guilty about things over which she had little control. We tried to console her and assure her that her boys would be cared for. She remained there for several months until the doctors felt that she was ready to face her world again.

My life went on after that experience, but my view of things had undergone a change. Before witnessing Mildred's illness, I easily saw the humorous side of life in most events. Now I grew much more sober. I had been whining and bellyaching about the austerity of my life. I had no clue about what was going on in the world around me. Mildred recovered and was able to go on with her life, raising her children with love and patience.

Since entering the convent some nine years previously, I had never turned on a radio or read a newspaper. My life had been isolated from the troubles of the world, but now some truths about life began to emerge from this experience.

My conclusions included maxims that were probably evident to most people. They now became real for me. These newly learned truths were: Life is short and sometimes very tragic, and each day we are reminded of our finiteness. Mildred's suffering caused me to reflect on my own mortality. It made me realize anew what I really wanted out of life. I want to grow in my trust in God and in his plan for my life and for the lives of all I loved. I knew that he wants all of us to stay close to him. I believed that God is good and all knowing—nothing catches him by surprise, not the car out of control, the malignant tumor, the hurricane, or mental illness. He does not cause these things. So even as I wondered and questioned the cause for Mildred's illness, I knew that God knows and that in everything he is working all things toward good. He has all the facts; we know so little about the why and the how of any specific incident in our lives. I stopped asking that impossible question, *"Why is this happening to my sister?"* I traded that question for a belief that brought comfort, *"I trust that you are all good, Lord. I will probably never understand the answer to the question of why bad things happen to good people, but I will always trust that you will bring good from every event, if we place our trust in you."*

Jesus instructs us, "Do not be worried about anything." Jesus knows about this life and its pains. If he had remained in heaven, perhaps I would not have paid as much attention to this advice. However, because God stepped down to earth and wrapped himself in human flesh and human problems, I knew that I could trust him even in those events that I couldn't understand. I realized that I could not control the future. I couldn't even add one day to my life. While I knew that I had to take responsibility for who I am and work to make my life the best that I could, I had to remember that I can only control my life up to a point. After that, I have to trust in God's love and mercy.

Chapter 18
Some Lessons Learned

My stay in Oakes lasted for four years. There are many great memories from those days spent there among people who were so supportive of our school and what we were trying to accomplish there.

Of the many good people I remember, one little fellow, Billy, who holds a special spot in my heart. He was small for his age but he had a huge heart and brain. He absorbed learning like a super dried-up sponge. I remember he volunteered to memorize a very long poem, "The Leak in the Dike," for a school program for parents. He learned it in no time at all and when he finished reciting it at the program, there was not a dry eye in the house.

He was an altar boy and served with so much dignity when it was his turn to serve at Mass. One morning he was alone in serving, when the other boy did not show up. When it came time to change the big book of the Scripture from one side of the altar to the other, which was a practice in the old days before Vatican II, he bravely reached up high to the altar and picked up the heavy book together with its heavy wooden holder. As Billy began to bring it down, the book fell on his upturned face. Father McDonald, head bowed low, deep in prayer preparing to read the Gospel, failed to notice the boy struggling to find some way to get his job done. Billy was completely immobilized and blind with the weight of the book on his face. As we watched, we saw the red of embarrassment rise from his neck on up. There were not many people present but all felt the intense need to laugh at the comic situation. Finally, Father noticed the boy's dilemma, came to his rescue, and lifted the Book to its proper place.

Later, Billy told me that he didn't feel too bad about what happened until he looked out and saw everyone laughing. I had to admit to him that I was sorry but that I was one of them. He grinned and said, "You were the first person I looked at and I saw that you were laughing so hard the tears were running down your cheeks. You better do some penance for that!" He had a great sense of humor besides all of his other outstanding qualities.

I could not keep Billy supplied with enough material to satisfy his hungry mind. I asked his parents just before the Christmas holiday if they thought it would be good if he advanced to the next grade. At first, they were a little leery because of his size, but finally they decided to give it a try. During Christmas vacation, he studied all the material that the next class had covered during the first part of the year. By January, he was ready and he had no trouble keeping up with his new class. Recently, I learned that he became a very successful lawyer and that he died of cancer at a very early age.

Another great boy, Bobby, is often in my memories. This boy loved school too, but he had a hard time with math. Try as he might, he just couldn't seem to learn the multiplication tables. His classmates took turns helping him but he often became very discouraged.

One weekend, this innocent boy was riding in the family car with his older brother. They rode along on a gravel road and the car overturned. Death came upon this child in an instant. On that terribly blue Monday morning, I met my class with deep mourning in my heart. Bobby was the first student that I had ever lost through death. It was so hard to counsel the children, though most of them had parents who knew how to approach tragedy from a faith outlook. While we discussed how much we would miss Bobby, one child raised his hand and sagely offered, "Now, Bobby knows all of his multiplication tables without any trouble. He knows a whole lot of things that we will have to learn the hard way." This response brought a smile to everyone's face and hope to these young maturing hearts as well as to their grieving teacher. As time passed, we could not forget Bobby and we remembered the joy he had brought to our lives.

If someone had asked me at that time what the town of Oakes was like, I would have had to answer that I did not have a clue as to most of the population, to its extent or what stores it contained. I only knew those few who were my students and their parents.

All I remember about the town is the hospital where we attended daily Mass. In 1930, a distant cousin of our family, W.T. Noonan, sold his lavish home to a group of Benedictine nuns from Canada so that they might transform it into a 20-bed hospital. It had changed hands many times in the years since. While I lived in Oakes, the Irish Presentation Sisters from Aberdeen owned and operated the hospital.

Our superior, Sister Geraldine, arranged to have our groceries delivered to our door so we never had to go shopping. I don't remember just how she arranged it, but two of our young students, Patricia and Tom, often pulled their little red wagon to the convent loaded down with the groceries that we needed each week. It seemed those two thought it was a great privilege to be of service to their teachers.

My students were not always angels. They did get into trouble from time to time. One example of this happened one night after classes were over. Several girls and boys were playing outdoors, waiting for their parents to pick them up. One or two of them got the bright idea of throwing pebbles at the cars that passed by the school. I don't know how many motorists they angered, but one lady stormed into my classroom holding on to the ears of two mischief-makers she had caught in the act.

She was furious as she exploded into my room shouting, "Are these two brats your students?"

Well, that was definitely the wrong tack to take with me. As calmly as I could, I asked her to release her hold on the two children. Then I told her that these two children were indeed my students but that they were certainly not brats. She calmed down and I let her explain why she was so angry. She said, "I am just passing through your town. I am shocked to find such behavior from students who attend a Catholic school. I have never come across this kind of behavior in my hometown of St. Paul."

"Oh, really?" I thought.

After hearing her story, I assured her that I would see to it that they were adequately and justly punished. I thanked her for calling their misdeed to my attention. The lady left in a much quieter mood than she had entered. I took care of the students in my own way and they assured me they would never do anything like that again. These children learned so easily from their mistakes that a simple chore assigned to them as punishments was all that was necessary. For the next week, my chalkboards and erasers were always clean and ready for use.

The next day I asked the students about their ideas

concerning respect for other people's property. They seemed to know just how important it is because they didn't like others to steal or damage their property. Then, I asked the offenders if they would like to share their story relating to this so that all could learn from it.

The braver of the two got up with a bit of a swagger in his manner, saying with pride in his voice, "You should have heard Sister stick up for us when that lady called us brats!"

All the students cheered. Just then, there was a loud knock on the door. Everyone became suddenly very silent. The person who had just delivered the speech with the conclusion about what was important about the pebble incident whispered, "Wow! What if that is *her* at the door?"

As I made my way to answer the knock, I whispered, "You mean, what if that is *she* at the door?"

Sure enough, there she stood with two big buckets of ice cream, paper plates, spoons and cookies. She said that she wanted to apologize for calling the children names. I invited her in and she treated all the children with her goodies. She talked to the children in a totally different tone than she had the night before. The children, of course, were pleased at this unexpected outcome of their mischief.

After she left, I asked the children what they had learned from this incident. One impish young boy assumed, "Get more pebbles and watch for rich ladies' cars!"

Loud, good-natured laughter followed and I knew that they had learned more than respect for property that morning.

In 1954 my brother, Ralph (Sam) invited me to his upcoming wedding. He was engaged to a young teacher, Marilyn Palensky, from Crete, North Dakota. I had thought Sam was a confirmed bachelor because he was nearly 33 years old. Marilyn was much younger. They planned to be married in the small town of Stirum, which was not far from Oakes.

My superior told me to call Valley Center to get permission to attend the wedding. I wouldn't have needed the phone to hear Mother Provincial's reply. She yelled her objection so loud it hurt my ears and my heart. "You know that we don't attend such things as weddings. Why do you even ask when you know it will never be allowed?"

I had no answer for that but my brother was completely mystified that I could not attend a wedding in a Catholic church so near to the convent. He asked, "Even Jesus is said to have gone to weddings and he even performed his first miracle there, didn't he?"

Again, I had no answer but I agreed with him in my heart and wished him and Marilyn a happy life. Indeed, Marilyn was a welcome addition to the family. She brought the somewhat roguish personality of my brother under her gentle influence. The Verona community knew of his many youthful escapades as they did of my two younger brothers, Gene and Fritz. Sam was just as full of pranks as they, but now that he had become a man, he put away most of his childish behaviors, thanks to Marilyn.

By 1955, my brother Fritz married Martha Werlinger from Rapid City. Another child was born to my brother Don and his wife Kitty. They named her Monica in my honor. I was mightily pleased about that. They wanted me to be her godmother but my community did not allow us that privilege because we were not in a position to care for a child's upbringing should something happen to the parents. By this time, Gene and Rosemary were the parents of two children, Mark and Patricia. Lynda Ann brought the number of children up to four for Lil and Aaron. Sam and Marilyn had welcomed a son, Owen into the world. Mom and Dad were acquiring a good number of grandchildren.

And in that year, 1955, our parish in Oakes celebrated its 50th anniversary. I remember helping to prepare skits to celebrate its history. This is what is recorded of that event in the Oakes Centennial History, page 123.

"Over the years, the local newspaper reported plays and pageants presented by the children of Saint Charles. In 1955, on the fiftieth jubilee of the parish, they put on what the *Oakes Times* termed "a historical and reminiscatory skit." That same school year witnessed the largest graduation in the history of the parish school, as nineteen eighth-graders received their diplomas."

We did put on many wonderful operettas that included a role for every child. We had only a small stage in the basement level of the school but we always put up appropriate props, sometimes with backdrop scenery that we had spent long hours projecting on paper before painting. A little first grade girl, Karen, stole the show during one Christmas play. Her only line was, "Oh, Jesus has come!"

Karen always jumped up and down while she said, "Oh, Jesus has **came!**" The audience loved it! I always wondered if Karen fully realized just what a great statement she made in acknowledging the importance of Jesus' coming in our lives.

Also, in the summer of 1955, I went back to Great Falls for another summer of study. I took a course in logic from a priest who was a DP (Displaced Person) from some European country. He opened my eyes to topics that I had never known existed. With the myriad of examples that he gave, I learned to be more vigilant about detecting inconsistencies and ambiguities in my own and other people's writings. I studied hard to ace that class as well as taking a heavy course in US History. I also enrolled in a class in Russian History. Several weeks after this class had started, our professor became ill. The dean asked me to take over the teaching of that class. I did that for about 2 weeks until the professor recovered. That wonderful experience boasted my spirits. My lifestyle of being pushed into tasks beyond my capabilities prepared me well to meet this challenge. Until the professor returned, I enjoyed being stretched in a new direction.

In the spring of 1956, my superiors decided that our community would no longer staff the school in Oakes. With deep regret, we packed up all of our belongings and bid goodbye to many wonderful people that we had come to know in this community. Just recently, I found this comment in the "Oakes Centennial History" on page 123 concerning the closing of our school:

"The memories linger: of music recitals and plays; of Christian values taught; of academic achievements; of picnics and games and childish pranks; of nuns, both kindly and stern; of an alternate source of education welcomed perhaps more in its birth than in its demise. It was an institution that made a significant contribution to the education of the youth, now grown, who knew Oakes and Saint Charles School as the ambience of their formative years."

It was about this time that our community started to change from the traditional French peasant headdress to a more modern one as well as a modified dress. It was quite a relief not to have to wear that starched headdress that was so cumbersome. Our dress was also much less complicated but it was still very warm in the summer time.

That summer I attended the College of St. Francis in Joliet, Illinois. I had an easy summer as I took only two courses: US History Since the Reconstruction and one that I loved: Christ: The Moral Ideal.

This course helped me realize that the true core of Jesus' moral teachings went far beyond rules and regulations. The Commandments, rules and regulations are guides to live out Christian life. They were not the means of salvation. If I broke one of them, I would not lose my salvation, but it would diminish the closeness of my relationship with Jesus. Jesus gives salvation as a pure gift to us without any cost to us whatsoever. He loved me, saved me, gave me this incredible "new life" while I was

130

yet a sinner. I didn't have to do anything to receive that gift except to admit I could not save myself and accept the fact that He is my Savior and Lord. Jesus wants my whole heart to serve him out of love, not out of fear of going to hell. It became clearer to me that I had to internalize Jesus' teachings and it would prove to be a lifelong task. God would be constantly there with the Holy Spirit to transform me from that old way of life to the new life that Jesus gave me by His death and resurrection. This task had to start with the right image of God. I learned that if I believed that God's love and goodness are dependent on my own good actions, my walk with him would be joyless and minimal. If I truly understand his unconditional love, I will serve him with joyful love.

It was a very restful summer for me. My brother Fritz and his wife, Martha, came to Joliet one weekend from their home in Chicago to treat me to a wonderful visit to their city. It was the first time I really got a good look at what a big city was like. Fritz took me for an evening drive along Lake Michigan. Even at that late hour, the cars were whizzing by at a terrifying speed. I couldn't imagine where everyone was going. Their speed indicated to me that emergencies were calling them out to pass every car in front of them.

I spent one day with my parents after my retreat. My superiors said my next assignment was teaching at St. Benedict School in Walaha, North Dakota. When I told my dad where I would be teaching, he was horrified. He said he had been to Walaha a few times in his roadwork and it was a wild town. He didn't think that I should go anywhere near that place. He really didn't understand that I did not choose the place. My superiors sent me there.

Chapter 19
Heading for Walaha

As we came down the last hill on our approach, Walaha spread out like a beautiful little town in a small valley. The school looked relatively new, and for once, the convent was in a large separate house from the school. It looked like a regular residence rather than the usual cold, brick buildings where I had previously lived.

On the first day of school, I stood at the door of the classroom welcoming each child as they entered. Suddenly, I felt something stab my back. At the same time a low, malicious voice said, "Stickum up and give me the gold from your teeth!"

My dad's warnings about the dangers of living in this town immediately came to mind. Nevertheless, I turned to find a grinning boy looking up mischievously at me. He laughed when he saw the look on my face. A dentist had replaced a damaged tooth with a false one edged with shining gold along the front margins. It was quite noticeable whenever I smiled. This was the beginning of many unexpected and happy times spent at this school. The harmless bandit, Timothy, and many more like him, made the next seven years a memorable time in my life.

Walaha's population contained at least two groups of people. This town was not far from an Indian reservation. Many people of Indian heritage had left the reservation and had taken up residence in Walaha. For the most part, these good people were poor and lived in the poorer part of town, "across the tracks," so to speak, from those who had more money. The children of both segments attended our school. They were often at odds with one another, jealous or condescending in their attitudes depending on their outlook. As teachers, we took extra care not to show favoritism to any one person, as we realized that it could easily make it very difficult to reach all people.

Through the years there at St. Benedict, I came to love all my students, many of whom would tear at my heartstrings. A little one of Indian descent came to my fourth grade class in the fall of 1960. I knew nothing about his family. Soon I learned that this little lad, Ron, had four or five older brothers who were constantly "raising hell" all over town. Ron thought that he must follow in their footsteps.

As the days of school went on, I came to know Ron very well. He was ever on the alert to see if I paid more attention to the "other" students than I did to him. He constantly did things in an attempt to annoy me. When he got too out of hand, I finally told him that he had to stay after school. He pretended to be hurt, angry and rebellious.

After school, I asked him to clean the erasers or wash the blackboard, or some other little chore. He took up the task always with the same words: "I really hate your guts!" I never took his tirades personally. I knew that he was a troubled child who needed to know that someone saw some good in him. I did.

I often brought some extra goodies such as fruit and a sandwich from the convent because I thought that he often looked very hungry. After school I left him to his task, telling him that I had to consult with one of the other nuns, casually adding, "There is some lunch left on my desk. You are welcome to have it if you want."

Invariably, he replied, "I suppose you are trying to poison me so that you will be rid of me." I laughed and told him that I didn't know what I would do if I didn't have him around.

When I returned after several minutes, the lunch was gone and I found a little softer expression on Ron's face improved by some much-needed nourishment. Still, unable to shake his need to look notoriously bad, he would insolently ask if I had more punishments for him.

I soon found out that he liked staying after school. He would always do something during the day in hopes that I would make time to keep him after school. He seemed to enjoy being in school but yet he frequently repeated, "I know that you hate my guts."

I always replied, "Ron, why would I hate you? You are not a bad boy. You just do bad things once in awhile. I could never hate you for that. You are a very normal boy."

Other students did not always receive good nourishment at home. Those were the days before our schools served hot lunches to all, whether they could afford it or not.

One of those wonderful boys was a lad by the name of Denny. He often came to school without being washed or having clean clothes. Sister Paulette was his teacher. She told us that one day she took him into the bathroom to wash his little hands before school started. She noticed that when the layers of dirt were removed that his skin was covered with a serious rash. She asked him what had caused that. He did not know. Sister began to question him about the foods that he may have eaten that might cause this allergic reaction.

"What did you eat for breakfast?" she asked.

"Eggs," he replied.

'And for supper?" she continued.

"Eggs," was his answer.

"How about for lunch yesterday?"

"Eggs!"

Sister Paulette sagely replied, "I think it's the eggs."

In later years, Denny got in trouble, as did a number of other students. They were sent to the Reformatory in Mandan, North Dakota. Once those sent there experienced the good food, the good beds, the relatively quiet of that school, they kept going back there even after they had served their time. They came back to Walaha, did the bad deed again and waited to be sent back to a place that had better living conditions than they found at home. It was often said, "St. Benedict is the prep school for the Reformatory." This was not because we didn't do our best to help the poor of the parish but more because some parents were confirmed alcoholics and poor in other respects.

Whenever it did not insult those proud little people who came to our school each day hungry and in need of love, we sent them over to the convent with a note to our Superior, Mother Martin, who was also our housekeeper and cook. The note stated that this little messenger needed some food. Mother Martin was a roly-poly nun with a heart as big as she was. She would find a way to make children feel loved as she took them into her kitchen and into her wonderful heart. Many people in Walaha to this present day remember the goodies they consumed from her generous hand and the love they experienced in her clean, cozy kitchen.

I had a very large class of fourth graders that year of 1960. There were about 40 students, if I remember correctly. It was great to have to teach only one class but in that class were children at various stages of maturity and intelligence. It took all my energy to see to their every need. A few of those children, I think, came from abusive homes. I didn't know much about looking for signs of that as I did in later years when this phenomenon became more known. I had students that could have been real discipline problems had it not been that God had given me a great love for children and the gift of patience. It didn't take long to let all my students know that I loved them but that I would not tolerate disorder in the classroom unless it came from a learning situation. Most of the students, as far as I can remember, appreciated that and we got along well together.

In 1959, my brother, Gene, was home for a short vacation from his work for the government in the Pacific Islands. My mother asked him to bring her to visit me. It was a short visit, but again, they both filled me in on the family happenings. Gene's wife had given birth to a daughter, Barbara Jean at the beginning of the year. Lil had divorced Aaron. Sometime later, she met and married Heinz Jeschkeit who was the father of a three-year old daughter, Cynthia Ann. Now Lil was the mother of five children.

Lil's divorce was very painful for both Lil and my mother. Though the church adamantly opposed the breakup of families, mom knew that circumstances sometimes made it necessary to look to the spirit of the law rather than the letter. I was amazed at the wonderful non-judgmental attitude of my mother in this regard.

Don and Kitty added another son, David Paul, to their family in February of 1957. I had missed out on many of these happy occasions. Mom hesitated to write too many details because my letters were still censored by my superiors. Mom counted up all the grandchildren to a new total of twenty-three, with her youngest daughter Mildred giving her the greatest number with her seven beautiful children.

We had a great visit, yet before long, they had to return home because Gene had many things to do before he left for the Islands again. Mom was now sixty-eight years old. She had inherited some money when her older sister, Margaret, died. With that capital, she and dad bought a farm just one mile from Verona. Dad was in his element again, tilling the soil, caring for a few animals and harvesting his crops. Mom didn't like to leave him alone for too long. He was still healthy and actively farming at the age of seventy and he would continue well into his late eighties.

One of the things that brought much happiness to my mom was the return of my father to the Church. Before she left, she told me how that had come about during a time when a "mission" was held in our home parish. A priest came to preach the gospel for several days in the parish. People left their farm work, if they could, to attend at least one service each day.

Mom said that somehow or other, dad had decided it was time to serve the Lord again, but he wanted to do it all on his own. Mom was surprised when dad quit his work early each day, dressed up and left the house without telling her where he was going. The next day the same thing happened. Finally, on the third day dad said, "Bessie, I have been trying to go to confession for the last two days, but the priest is never around when I get there. Can you help me locate him?"

Mom was overjoyed. She went with him to town after she had called to make an appointment. She waited in the car while dad went in to set things straight with the Lord. Finally, dad came out of the parish house with his head down and with a sorrowful look on his face.

Mom asked with worry in her voice, "What happened? Are you all right?"

Dad replied, "The priest said it is much too late for me. I am bound for hell!"

Mom was aghast. "That is ridiculous. Let me go talk to that priest! We will see who's going to hell."

Dad started to laugh. "Calm down, Bessie. I was just trying to get your Irish up. You are so beautiful when you get angry."

"You rascal. You had me going there. That priest would have been mighty sorry if I had gotten a hold of him," Mom laughed.

With that last story, she and Gene left me to thank God for his great mercy and for allowing me to have such a great visit with them.

Chapter 20
Joys and Sorrows in Walaha

The next year, the principal, Sister Mary, asked me to move into the fifth grade classroom right along with my students from the previous year. No one else wanted to tackle that big class with that number of rambunctious students. I was very happy to go along with them. The same occurrence came the following year until that class graduated from our school in the fall of 1963.

During my seven years of teaching at St. Benedict, teachers came and went on to other schools. Sometimes there was hardly time to get to know each one very well. Sister Mary replaced Mother Martin as superior of the convent while she retained her position as principal of the school. She was tiny, quiet, easily amused, and gentle with the authority given to her. She never lorded it over anyone.

An enjoyable memory of her happened on the first day of school. Besides her other duties, she taught the first grade. Sometimes, the first day of school is very scary for the little ones. On this particular day, one such new student did not want to stay in school. Out the door he ran, with little Sister Mary right on his heels. Silhouetted against the light coming through the glass doors of the school entrance, she gently scooped up the boy who was only a little smaller than she was. As I happened to look down the long hall at that scene, I could see little arms and legs stretching and straining to get out of her grasp as he hollered at the top of his lungs. She hung on until the boy decided he had met his match. Back to school he went, to settle down to learn the great lessons of life that his sweet teacher presented.

The next year, another nun came to teach the first grade students. What a poor replacement she turned out to be. She had been raised in a very legalistic home as I came to learn when her mother came for a visit. Her mother was a nervous wreck, tormented by worries of sin as she labored under the false idea that she must earn her salvation. Nothing she did was ever good enough. Sin dominated her life. She had passed on to her daughter, Sister Dolorosa, these same guilt-filled ideas. She never learned that Jesus wants us to fellowship with him – not with our sins.

Sister Dolorosa was a frantic perfectionist. If she fell short of what she thought was faultless, she was dejected and plagued with guilt. She needed to confess her sins almost every day, and then she was never certain that God had forgiven her. She suffered constantly from scrupulosity. She passed this need for perfection on to her little students. If they made an error on a paper they were coloring or writing, she insisted they erase it and start again. Sometimes the little ones were seen with tears streaming down their faces as they erased holes in their papers and then Sister had them start all over again. No little one needs a teacher like that.

Sister Mary Janelle came to take up a class one year. She was what I would call a low- maintenance friend. We didn't have to tiptoe around each other. We could say what we wanted without a single worry that our words would be taken wrong. Such friends are few and far between and our friendship has lasted to this day, though we seldom have the opportunity to meet. When we do, it is like no time or circumstances has changed in our lives. We just pick up where we left off. That's my idea of what true friends are like. I am grateful for that gift.

Surrounded by many good teachers, the years went by quickly. Problems popped up but nothing major that caused undue stress. Classroom discipline was easy for me.

It was not only the poorer students that had struggles. One boy in my sixth grade class, Peter, came from a great home where his parents apparently loved and cared for him. But his emotions as he approached puberty went wild. He suffered terribly from thoughts of going to hell because of all his "impure temptations." Many times during the day, he asked if he could wash his hands. He thought that ritual would cleanse the bad thoughts from his mind. He didn't want to go to communion each morning because he thought he was too sinful. I tried my best to assure him that Jesus wanted him to come to him. "I will commit a sin of sacrilege, if I do," he insisted.

"I will take all your sins upon me. If they are mortal, I will take the blame," I assured him.

"You would do that for me?" he asked incredulously.

"Absolutely, and Jesus did the same thing for you when he died on the cross. He took my sins, your sins and the sins of the entire world upon himself. Then God took Jesus' righteousness and gave it to all of us who believe in him," I counseled. "Jesus loved us so much he just traded places with us!"

Peace would return to him for a while but scruples would come back with a vengeance later. His parents finally had to take him for professional counseling. I prayed that he finally learned to live in the peace that Jesus came

143

to give us.

When Mother Martin had moved on to another convent, a little French nun, Sister Cajatun, came to do the cooking for the convent. She moved about quickly and always tried to serve up a delicious meal each evening. I made the mistake of telling her how much I liked her pasta dishes. From that day on, we got pasta in some form several times a week. My fellow sisters cautioned me not to mention any preferences again. They were sick of pasta.

We had an artist on our faculty one year. She loved to paint and her students did great work. Her only fault was her lack of order in her class and in her appearance. Paint covered her more than it did her canvas. The children loved Sister Charles and they flourished under her chaotic care. She also found time to author a small book that told tales of her life on the farm before she entered the convent. She illustrated all her stories with imaginative drawings.

About the year of 1961, I had been fitted with contact lens. That was a great blessing. The heavy lenses needed to correct my extremely myopic vision had been exasperatingly sliding down my nose for many years. With contacts, even though I had the same students, they looked brand-new to me. I could now see all their freckles, dimples and every twinkle in their eyes. It also helped me as I continued to teach music lessons each Saturday and each evening before the supper hour to piano students. Now I could see every staccato mark as never before.

Two sisters, Mary Lee and Valerie, talented piano students, came from the public school for music lessons on Saturdays. Later they went on to Nashville to seek fame and fortune with their talents. They had to work hard to find gigs and they learned perseverance from their experiences. Mary Lee decided to take up nursing and Valerie became the assistant chief of police in Nashville, while both still enjoyed their love of music.

In addition to giving music lessons, I was in charge of

the adult choir. I had learned a little from my experiences in Oakes but I was still very nervous. All of the adults were kind and cooperative. I found many good friends among them. One especially stands out among many others. Gloria was the mainstay of the choir with her rich alto voice. We remained friends all through my stay and in the years that followed as much as we were able.

Also in 1961 a hit-and-run driver killed my nephew, Robert, aged 7. What a blow to the family that was, but especially to my sister, Mildred, whose mental health was still very fragile. Since his funeral took place during my summer school sessions, I could not take time off to be with my sister because my superiors pushed me to obtain my degree. They promised that I could be with my sister as soon as summer school ended. I did spend time with the family but Mildred was back in the hospital recovering once again from a mental breakdown.

Her husband begged me to stay in any case. The family had grown in the years since I had seen them. Timothy Allen was 11, Ronald Anthony was 9, Janine Anne was 5, David Arnold was turning 4, Beverly Alice was 3, Patricia Arlyn was just 2 and baby Alan Arvid was not yet a year old. This was quite a responsibility for this young father to bear with his wife in severe depression. To help take away the sadness of the loss of Robert, their father, Roger, arranged to take the whole family including myself down the St. Croix River on a boat. During this lengthy excursion, he was able to express to me his bitterness about the accident that had taken his son's life and had put his wife back in the hospital. I tried to explain that God does not cause such tragedies and that we can't always understand why they happen. He made great efforts to understand as we continued to talk and watch the children enjoy the beauties of the scenes along the river. I prayed that the bitterness would not eat at his heart.

Earlier in that same year, I heard from my mother that

she and Dad were again grandparents. Michael Robert was born in Lisbon, ND. Gene and Rosemary now had a family of four children. Mom and Dad, both now in their seventies, counted twenty-four grandchildren.

I continued my studies each summer. By the year 1962, I graduated with honor, *Magna Cum Laude* with a BA degree. With my shaky college beginning in 1948, it had taken me fourteen summer sessions, five correspondence courses from the University of Washington and the University of North Dakota and several credits earned by taking exams in French and basic math to complete this degree.

Back in Walaha that year, I had those same students that had started out with me in fourth grade. They were now ready to move on to public middle school. Those children were like my very own. I hated to see them leave but my superiors decided that I too must move on. As the years went on, I always remembered those students and have wished to know if they had gone on to enjoy life and remain faithful to their life in Christ.

From Walaha, I went on to a totally new call on my life.

Book Four
Tramping Through Turmoil

Do not conform yourselves to this age but be transformed by the renewal of your mind, that you may discern what is the will of God, what is good and pleasing and perfect.
ROM 12:2

There is nothing permanent except change.
Heraclitus

Chapter 21
A New Challenge:
May 1963 – August 1966

Just before the school year ended in the spring of 1963, my provincial superior, Mother Ellen, announced an upcoming visit to our convent in Walaha. She had governing control over all the nuns of our community located in North Dakota. According to custom, at the official arrival of a higher superior, the whole community met to greet her. She was hardly in the door when she laid an authoritative hand on my shoulder. Taken by surprise, I jumped back nervously. From the extreme pressure of her hand on me, I wondered why she had singled me out from the group. The strained expression on her face suggested something serious was coming down. She hastily ducked into the parlor just off the entry and indicated that I should follow and close the door. My heart was in my throat and my knees were shaking. I did as she proposed, knowing full well that the other nuns had their eyes glued on us in obvious curiosity. Through the glass door, Mother Ellen waved them off and then she came abruptly to the point. "You have been chosen by the Mother General in France to be the new Mistress of Novices at Autumn Vale, Illinois. You will train all the young ladies that will enter the convent there from now on."

She caught me completely flatfooted. One would never dare tell a Superior what was going through my mind at that moment: *"Mother General is completely out of her mind...that crazy French lunatic! She doesn't even know anything about me."*

Unperturbed by my obvious anguish at her words, she continued, "You will leave here as soon as the school term ends. You will attend theology and scripture seminars at Notre Dame that will prepare you for this new work."

*"Now, isn't that generous of you? You are giving me **one** summer school? And that is supposed to prepare me for a job with such far-reaching consequences?"*

Yes, I asked and answered those questions only in my mind. No words came out of my mouth, because I knew, categorically, she would not listen to my reasons for objecting! I felt totally inadequate for this new task. I was tired of studies, tired of assignments that taxed me to the limit, tired of swimming upstream with every new assignment. I just wanted one summer to rest. However, she was adamant and would not listen to any of my misgivings. This was normal. All she had to do was command and I obeyed. *Goodbye dear friends in Walaha.*

Vatican II had called for reform in the life of the church. Convents needed to re-think their methods of bringing the "Good News" of the gospel to the world. There were some small, hesitant efforts made in our community to follow the ideas expressed in the Vatican II documents. I had read some excerpts of a document called

Perfectae Caritatis (The Perfection of Charity). I had been excited about seeing how this document would affect our convent life. I had hoped for some major changes in some of our antiquated community practices.

For example, this decree stated that convent rules should take into consideration and fit the physical and psychological needs of each person in regard to their life, work, and prayers. It should also fit the culture of the country where each convent is located.

We surely would have a long way to go to accomplish even this small task. French customs characterized many of our community's practices, which simply did not fit life in America. At our community meetings, I was never bashful about speaking my mind. It is never easy to accept changes to what people have always accepted as the best way to live. I began to think that perhaps God was asking me to be instrumental in that regard, but I never wanted to be the head of anything. That stupid desire had never entered my mind. Nevertheless, I had to submit. Off I went to study at Notre Dame when the school term ended.

Notre Dame was an exciting place at this time after Vatican II. The campus was full of people who seemed almost fanatic about all the changes going on in the church. A new development called the Charismatic Movement was in full swing here. This trend was focused in individuals like Kevin Ranaghan and his group of followers. Kevin was a founding member of a group called the People of Praise, an ecumenical Christian community. I was very leery of this and many other active groups. I was not used to hearing about nuns and others who spoke in tongues, who clapped and shouted during the liturgy, and who sang hymns to the accompaniment of electric guitars jazzing it up.

The whole atmosphere on that campus came as a cultural shock to me. That first summer those new and strange systems of thought that circulated about did not influence me all that much. I was intent on learning as much theology and Scripture as I could. My discernment of what was right and in accord with Scripture needed constant reinforcement. My own emotional upheavals and misgivings because of this new assignment often seemed to block my ability to listen to the Holy Spirit.

My provincial superior, Mother Ellen, was my companion during that first summer. Every seminar that I took, she attended also. She constantly reassured me that she would approve of all changes that would come about because of what we learned here.

We took several classes designed to help nuns adapt to the changes called for by Vatican II. One of the first things that we came to realize was the need to reevaluate all the rules of our community. Those rules, written in France during a time when Jansenistic ideas permeated the thinking of our founding nuns, definitely needed revision because they promoted ideas perniciously opposed to Christ's teachings as revealed in Scripture.

These ideas were subtly present in notions that implied that "If something is difficult then it has to be God's plan for us. If something is pleasant and joyful and will make one feel great about self, that is sinful." These were the rules about avoiding friendships, family ties, and the need for relaxation and recreation. This lead to the concept that all one had to do was listen to those in authority for they were called to be the voice of God for all members.

Erroneous conclusion: Community members did not need the Holy Spirit. They just needed to obey. This would guarantee that they were doing the will of God. The need to question, evaluate, review and reform were alien to such rules.

These standards were specifically evident in the rules that brushed aside subordinates' opinions, making that person feel unworthy and hopelessly submissive. I favored true humility but not for practices that made a person feel like a worm or worse. Christ came to teach us to know exactly who we are in him. We are children of God, brothers and sisters of Christ, temples of the Holy Spirit. This does not allow us to look upon ourselves as some worthless person who therefore goes about with a depressing attitude of defeat. Christ came to bring joy to us so that we could proclaim the glory and victory of his redemption. He calls us to be people who act like we fully realize that we have been saved. Mother Ellen and I soon realized that every rule in the book needed scrutinizing to weed out those that did not reflect Christ's ideals.

Chapter 22

Curious Customs and Troubling Traditions

Little by little, almost imperceptibly, Mother Ellen became as enthusiastic as I was about finding ways for our community to embody the ideals that Christ's life and messages proclaimed for his followers. She began to search all the campus bulletin boards for notices of lectures that might help us get a firm grip on how we ought to proceed.

One day, she came hurrying into my study cubicle at the library saying, "Sister Monica Rose, I think I have found just the right series of evening lectures to get us started on the exact track."

"That will be great. I am tired of searching book after book for ideas that will help me," I answered with a tired smile.

Reading from her scribbled notes, she went on to say,

"There is a lecturer who has studied the ideas of Fathers Karl Rahner, Hans Kung and Yves Congar. He will speak tonight to nuns and monks here on the campus about the call to renewal. We are going."

I had heard that those three theologians were some of the chief consultants to Vatican II. I had read a little about each one of them. "That sounds like a good place to start. We better take along a good supply of notepaper."

Many learned professors from various fields of knowledge gave excellent lectures nearly every evening somewhere on the campus. Mother Ellen agreed that we should take in every evening lecture that might provide insights about pursuing renewal in our community. Sometimes we came away disappointed because what was said flew right over both our heads.

The first night of the proposed lectures concerned the discovery of the Dead Sea Scrolls. These scrolls comprised hundreds of documents that were discovered between 1947 and 1956 in eleven caves near the ruins of the ancient settlement of Qumran near the Dead Sea.

As the lecture began, Mother Ellen whispered, "Maybe I was wrong. What do the Dead Sea Scrolls have to do with our community?'

"Let's just listen and see what this is all about," I whispered back.

As if reading our minds, the lecturer ventured, "I hope to show how the discovery of these documents will shed new light on the need for a serious reexamining of certain customs in all present day convents and monasteries."

Our professor went on to say, "These documents contain the history of the Jewish monasticism of the Essene monks of Qumran."

He told of their strictness and practices of abstinence. Some of the basic features of those communities called for members to be dressed alike, to live in one household, to participate in common prayers and work. There was great insistance on following a rigid set of rules covering every part of their lives."

Unable to resist, I whispered once again, "Those ideas sound a lot like our customs, don't they?'

Mother Ellen nodded as the lecture went on.

The professor pointed out that there is a world of difference between what Jesus taught and what these Jewish monks practiced.

Now I really sat up and began to scribble notes as fast as I could as he described the Essene way of life in the Qumran communities.

He explained that Jesus did not tell his followers to isolate themselves from the world, to cut themselves off from the people outside their communities in order to hold on to their so-called higher-ranking sinlessness. The Qumram wanted to isolate themselves from sinners. Jesus was not like them at all. He ate with sinners, went to weddings, mingled with people. Those Qumran monks regarded themselves as the only people who were repentant; they thought they had a better way of life. Everyone else outside was considered immoral. In contract to this, Jesus called all to change. This call did not come from God's anger but arose from his loving mercy.

Evening after evening the lecturer went on, pointing out the differences between what Jesus practiced in his own life and those ancient practices that had evidently come down from the Qumran communities and into some contemporary convents and monastaries. Jesus did not approve of sad faces. His day was not regulated by rules and silence. He did not require a vow of obedience from his disciples nor did he call for regular periods of prayer; instead, he advocated a life totally dependent on God, a perpetual *attitude* of prayer. In fact, his life had the hallmark of total freedom from the legalism of the religion of that day.

After the lectures, Mother Ellen and I talked for hours

about how we could encourage our community to follow the Jesus pattern of life rather than that of the Qumran which was based on principles so foreign to the example Jesus gives us in the Gospels.

Mother Ellen asked with tones of frustration in her voice, "How in the world am I going to explain these kind of changes to our superiors over in France?"

I answered, "Surely they are going through similar calls to renew as we are. Probably they will be far ahead on that score since many of the theologians that our lecturer mentions are from Europe."

Later I found out how wrong I was about that conclusion. Our French overladies were digging in their heels, firmly resisting change. When it comes to relinquishing power and control over people, leaders do not necessarily let go easily.

We were taking a class that promoted the idea of reading several modern novels that expressed Christian ideals and would illustrate those ideals in practice. I intended to use that appealing plan when I took up the task of preparing young women for taking religious vows. I resolved not to crush and break their spirits but to help them realize that they, like other Christians, are invited to transform their lives by "putting on the mind of Christ." To do that, I realized that I needed to study Scripture much more than I ever had, because in the Bible, Christ reveals who and what he is really like.

As the summer wore on, I began to develop a formation philosophy. *Look, cousin Jim, I learned something from you!* I needed this as the backdrop for the formation program that I intended to develop. Having Mother Ellen right there with me gave me courage to continue with this task that, at first, I had found so insurmountable.

My first resolve: I would give these young ladies the best preparation for embracing convent life that I could. I would give them the freedom to question everything. I didn't want them to develop into robots that weren't allowed to think on their own. Furthermore, they had to have a good education. They need never lie about their qualifications nor bluff their way through situations as I had. I wanted them to be aware of all their options so that they could freely choose the kind of life they wanted to dedicate to the Lord.

When the summer ended, we left Notre Dame for St. Magdalene's Novitiate in Autumn Vale, Illinois. There, about twenty-two young ladies greeted me as *Mother* Monica Rose. The title of mother did not bother me nearly as much as the title that the community bestowed upon me, "Mistress of Novices!" Could any title be more inappropriate for a nun?

The novitiate had previously been under the direction of an ultra-conservative nun. She had personally invented even more restrictive practices than Mother Gertrude had dreamed up for me when I had been in formation at Valley Center, North Dakota.

She had covered all the mirrors in the novitiate with towels (That was the practice in France, as I had personally witnessed). When I asked the postulants and novices if they knew the purpose of this phenomenon, they told me it was to prevent vanity. As I reached up and jerked every towel off those mirrors, loud cheers and hearty applause arose from this group leading my tour of the building. Almost every face told me that they had found this practice as foolish as I did. I won over most of my charges at that moment. However, as with every group, a few disagreed with what I had just done. They were loyal to their former mistress and their faces showed that they thought I was the devil incarnate. These few would cause me no end of trouble as time went on.

From that incident, I should have learned to be a bit more cautious and tactful in implementing any more changes that I thought were necessary. But, true to my natural impulsiveness, I managed to ruffle a good many feathers as I went along with my plans to update the novitiate and postulant training program. In fact, as time went on, I became more and more aggressive in my need for speedy changes. It was not that I was prone to innovations, but I knew life is not meant to be static. Life in Christ leaves us open to new thoughts and new ways of proclaiming the gospel truths. With God, there is never a last word about how he leads people to the full truth.

Soon, I began to hear the first faint rumblings of disapproval from some of the very conservative members of the community. When they observed the novices reading novels, they gasped in horror. I hardly took notice of it. I was still so naive. I didn't realize that it did no good to stir up trouble about things that were relatively unimportant. I was not wise enough to pick and choose the worthy battles. "Onward and upward" became one of my mottos along with another: "Love will find a way." These mottos sounded good, but when push came to shove, they would not save me from the wrath that was to come.

St. Basil's Benedictine Abbey, College, and High School for men was located just a few miles from our convent. I started negotiating with the brilliant priests of the Abbey for some practical way to give my charges the best possible education. A visiting priest, coming to our convent once or twice a week to teach the novices, would not accomplish my goals for their education. After many consultations with the Abbot and Prior of St. Basil, our young ladies were the first to be admitted into that all-male college as full time students. Instead of one or two priests coming to St. Magdalene's Novitiate, all the novices and postulants would go each and every day to St. Basil's College or the High School.

What an uproar that caused. The boys and the seminarians both in the high school and the college levels were delighted. My fellow nuns, especially some of the older ones, were outraged. I went ahead, full steam. The Abbott was all for it; he contended that the presence of the novices and postulants would help the men learn some much needed lessons in gallantry.

The novices were in every debate that came up in their classes and their professors told me that they could really hold their own. Some very handsome and intelligent males challenged these young ladies to stick to their intent on becoming nuns. I thought it was better that they meet this challenge head-on while they were still in training rather than later on after they had taken vows. Some of the more conservative novices and postulants did not like the idea of mingling with men. They may have entered the convent to avoid them. If this were truly the case, I knew that they would either chose to leave or they would learn to adjust in a healthy, beneficial manner. Life is full of contrasts and mixtures and they would see plenty of that in their participation in campus life.

The canonical novices took classes in philosophy, theology and in Scripture as they were in the last stages of preparing to take their vows. The other novices and postulants were allowed to take whatever classes they needed to work toward their high school diploma or their degree. I took many of those classes right along with them when I had the time. We formed many friendships with the priests, students, and seminarians of St. Basil.

About this time, I received news of another tragedy that struck the family of my sister, Mildred. Through a strange accident, Patricia Aryln, the seventh child of the family, suffered the loss of one of her eyes. There seemed no end to the sorrows coming their way. Patricia was eventually fitted with an artificial eye and she adapted very well to this new condition. Mildred, though shaken by this ordeal, was able to cope and stay with her family. That word was very good news.

Chapter 23
Change and Chastisement

Although friendships were still suspect in many nuns' eyes, I formed an enjoyable and beneficial camaraderie with one of our nurse-nuns who headed the surgery department at the hospital. Sister Dorothy was super-skilled in nursing, and she had a marvelous outgoing personality. She held the admiration of all the doctors and nurses who were in her sphere of work. In chapel, she may have appeared with head bowed and her arms hidden in the massive sleeves of her habit, but there was nothing subservient about her as she went about her other activities.

She had found an unused room on the upper floor of her surgery wing. Whenever she had a spare moment from her busy hospital duties, she spent her time decorating and furnishing it as an oasis where she could rest, pray and relax after her long hours in surgery. Her doctor friends made frequent gifts to keep her refrigerator well stocked with snacks and wine. She found discarded easy chairs, colorful decorations, soft lighting, a record player and many other accoutrements to liven up her self-made retreat. She invited me to join her whenever I needed to get away from my stressful work of constantly fighting battles to change hearts chained to the slavery of legalism to the freedom of walking in the Spirit.

On many an evening, I would join her for long discussions on the changing face of convent life. As a nurse who was used to dealing with well-educated, mature people of the medical profession, she was professional and yet easy-going. She often chose to bend the rules of community living so that she could be with patients before and after their surgeries. She expressed the hope that future nurses from our convents would not be so uptight in their need to observe every jot and tittle of our rulebook when those in need required services. Some considered her "lax" in her observance of the rule. I found her delightfully professional and religiously at ease in her commitments to her Lord, her patients and her community.

On a late evening, while I was visiting with her, a doctor rang up to tell her that he had a suspicious maternity case and needed her presence immediately. She invited me to come along with her so that I could witness what was going on. I had never been in the surgery department before.

On arriving there, the doctor said that a husband had come in saying that his wife's water had broken and that she was in labor. She was one of the doctor's regular patients, though he admitted that he had not seen her for several months. He was almost positive that she had created a false psychological pregnancy. He had set her up in the delivery room. He needed two assistants to witness his procedure. He could find no one else he trusted more than Sister Dorothy at this late hour of the night.

Sister Dorothy told me to come with her so we could

both scrub up. I reminded her that I was not a nurse! She said that all the hospital needed was another witness, so I scrubbed and gowned, delighted to be part of this extraordinary happening.

The young lady moaned and cried, writhing in pains that seemed intense and frequent. Her belly was swollen, hugely distended. The doctor soothed her and began to give her a light anesthetic to relax her. Right before my astonished eyes, as soon as she lost control of her muscles, her belly deflated like a punctured balloon. His analysis had been correct. This lady had wanted a baby so badly that she made her body, her own mind and her husband believe she was expectant. The doctor, Sister Dorothy and I went as a team to inform her husband that, indeed, he was *not* a father. At first, he thought something had gone wrong during the delivery, and after the doctor showed him a book that outlined this rare occurrence, he admitted that his wife had some mental problems. The doctor assured him that she would get the help she needed there at the hospital.

All through this incident, Sister Dorothy had been truly professional. Away from her responsibilities, she was lighthearted and delightfully comic. She never seemed to be plagued with guilt feelings. If she had to miss a prayer session to tend to her duties, her duties became her prayers. She always seemed carefree and at ease, joyful in her service to others. When she knew that she would be off duty, she might, at times, indulge in a wee glass of wine. Fortunately, on this night she had imbibed only a soft drink.

When I came to her hideout, which "the powers that be" had not yet discovered, she encouraged me to discard my shoes, take off my headdress, and prop up my tired feet on a footstool. My days were difficult because of my need to carefully prepare my daily lessons on convent living to the young nuns. I had no former models to follow; I was pioneering in new territory. I spent many hours reading, studying, praying, and consulting with others having the same responsibility both by phone conversations and by letters.

Sister Dorothy was generous, sharing her supply of wine with me. I found this a real haven in times of stress. Long after midnight, rested and relaxed, I found my way back through the long, darkened halls of the hospital to the still darker halls of the novitiate, only occasionally *slightly* tipsy from more than one glass of her relaxing wine. I never imbibed any more than I had when I had been in France visiting one convent after another with the Mother General.

To be sure, I often forgot to first seek the Lord in these times of trouble. I was using this "den of iniquity,"' as it later came to be known, as a refuge and an escape. Still, I never thought the Lord begrudged me this period of relaxation and new experiences such as we had gone through together with the pediatrician and the woman with the false pregnancy.

After an experience like that, how I wished that I could call or write my mother to share some of the things that were happening in my life, but I did not have that freedom. Such an experience would have totally surprised her as it did me.

Mom still kept up her correspondence with me. She was alone most of the time since my brothers and sisters were all settled in their own lives. In the summer, Dad was out working in his beloved fields. Mom wrote copious notes about family milestones. She always wrote to me when she acquired a new grandchild. Gene's family had grown by two more girls, Roberta Ann born in 1963, and Maria Elizabeth in 1966. Mildred and her husband also added two more girls to their family, Elizabeth Alvera, born in 1963, and Monica Amy, born in 1966. Dad, who was now seventy-six years old, said: "Now, Mom, we have twenty-eight grandchildren. One of those has been taken away by death. Do you think our kids will give us any more?"

"That should just about do it!" concluded Mom. (They

were in for a big surprise seven years later.)

Each summer I continued my studies in theology and Scripture at Notre Dame. Mother Ellen came to Autumn Vale to replace me during that time. During my second and third years, the criticism toward me became stronger and more venomous. Mother Ellen started to backtrack her approval of the way I was training the novices. Rumors of my visits to Sister Dorothy's "barroom" came back to haunt me. I was not without blame. I had given certain spying nuns some real ammunition with which to attack me. They seized that ammunition and they held me in their sights. They were waiting for just the right moment to ambush me.

When I returned at the end of one summer, the novices and postulants were really in need of a break from their daily routine. The family of one of them had offered to let us use their secluded cabin on a nearby lake. Mother Ellen gave her permission for us to spend a week there. I had not yet learned to avoid asking for too many "privileges." The novices were getting ready and wanted to pack suitable clothing, such as shorts and swimwear, for enjoying the beach. Since this was not covered by any "rule," I thought I had better clear it with Mother Ellen. She was horrified that I would even ask. The novices were to stay in their long habits and out of the water!

I mulled over that command for a few days. Why would it be wrong to enjoy God's great gift of water and sunshine? I decided to forget to tell the novices about Mother Ellen's edict on the matter of clothing. I told them to wear their habits until we reached the seclusion of the cabin. Then they could don their shorts and swimwear when no one was around.

One late afternoon, Sister Dorothy appeared with two doctors and their wives. They had brought along a grill, steaks, all kinds of picnic foods and a cooler filled with cold soft drinks and beer. They thought they would treat us as we were nearing the time to get back to regular convent living.

Believe it or not, I had never tasted a meal from a grill before. The visitors handled everything. I had some qualms of conscience when some of the novices helped themselves to the beer. I did nothing to stop them even though I could see that a couple of the very conservative novices frowned with outright disapproval about everything that was going on. I could see no evil as long as there was no overindulgence. After our delicious meal, the doctors set off a few fireworks to end a very enjoyable day.

The next day, our last day of vacation, Mother Ellen and some of her cohorts decided to visit us unannounced. When Mother saw the novices splashing and cavorting happily in the lake, she screamed at them like a scalded banshee. We were ordered to pack up and return to the novitiate immediately. I had disobeyed. It was my fault. But I was glad we had been able to have a few days of fun in the sun. The novices and postulants felt more pity for me than for losing their last day at the beach. I reminded Mother Ellen that I had told her that I was not qualified for this job. From the look of disgust on her face, I think she finally agreed with me.

Life again became very stressful for me. Father Owen, a Benedictine priest from the nearby Abby, was my mentor and counselor. He was wise, deeply spiritual, skillful with people and adept at handling irate nuns. I was often one of those. Whenever a letter came to me from France scolding me for some reported departure from the "old ways," I would fire off a scathing reply telling them in so many words to mind their own business; this was America, not France and we had to do things differently here.

One of their greatest concerns was that I allowed the novices to question every custom and rule of the community. Mother General ordered me to stop that practice; therefore, subordinates and those in training had no right to ask why certain senseless rules were in the books. They were to obey without question. It was as if Mother General in far off France received the last word on how the convent world operates. She permitted no healthy questions that might allow for growth and change.

I could see why such training was necessary for someone who was joining the military, but for those who were serving the Lord out of love, the idea that they had to be broken in spirit did not seem right to me. There is a right and a wrong way to "have that broken spirit" that total dependence on God that Christian life requires.

Before mailing my red-hot letters of protest, I always took them to Father Owen for his suggestions. He would calm me down and help me reword them in a more humble way without backing down from sound principles. He saved me from many foolish mistakes. He was not totally able to dampen my anger at times, and his efforts did not always save me from many cruel barbs hurled by the nuns who opposed me. (These nuns were not evil; they were just scared.)

Looking back, I can see that I was not sensitive to the feelings of the older nuns who, for years, had followed a certain pattern of living, had worn the same peasant dress, and had followed orders blindly. It must have been horrendous for them to think about wearing shorter skirts, shaving their legs and exposing their gray hairs to the world after having all of that hidden from sight for so long.

Since my recent education had been so sketchy and obtained in the turbulent atmosphere of Notre Dame, I did come back from there with some half-baked theological notions. Priests from the Abbey helped me cull out some of the crazy ideas that floated about that campus. Some ideas withstood the scrutiny of Scripture and common sense; others had to be discarded. The Spirit of God seemed to be opening so many windows that the ensuing draft caused "sacred cows" to fly about, shattering stale as well as some wholesome practices.

I witnessed many strange events at Notre Dame. Still, that is where Mother Ellen told me to get ideas for renewal. At Notre Dame, there were groups of priests who were in and some who had stepped out of their calling. There were nuns who chased after both groups, nuns who married them, or were openly living with them. There were couples that pretended to have platonic relationships that did not violate their vows of celibacy. It was all very confusing to this country bumpkin who was trying her best to avoid falling into any of those traps.

Soon the older novices were ready for profession and new young ladies asked for entrance to our convent. I had a great group of eager aspirants who, I believed, would one day be great servants of the Lord. Then in early fall of 1966 came a letter from France demanding that I come there to explain my methods to the Superior General. It was also the time for the General Chapter, a meeting to elect new leaders and discuss the future of the community.

I made this dreaded trip to France with several other nuns, representatives of different regions here in America. I was 37 years old and felt twice that age. One of those traveling with me was my ex-superior, Mother Patricia. She was serving as an American counselor to the Mother General in France. Once we reached the motherhouse in France, she took me aside and warned me to be submissive. She said that plans were well underway to transfer the novitiate back to North Dakota to our new provincial house, Maryhill, located in the country outside of Valley Center. I was appalled.

"Why move the training center back to this place where they will have no access for an excellent high school and college education? I asked.

"Postulants and novices need training in convent life. They need to learn to help out the older sisters, to help care for our extensive new building, and be secluded from outside influences," she rejoined.

Oh, sweet Jesus, where is this all leading? Are you behind this? I don't think so!

I anticipated the same old way of educating the young nuns with such a move to North Dakota. Such plans meant there would be no great professors to help me in the formation program. I couldn't do it alone and I knew that it would result in again falsifying records to get nuns out in the field that they would be inadequately prepared to face. I told Mother Patricia that I would never consent to be in charge of training if the novitiate locale was changed. She said, "So be it! We can get someone else to be in charge." There was little warmth or compassion in her voice.

I knew then it was the beginning of the end of my days as a molder of future nuns. I feared for the future of the wonderful young ladies who were still in training. They would not fare well in a restrictive life-style that would stifle their gifts and crush their spirits.

When I was called in for my interview with the Mother General, I knew that she already had made up her mind not to listen to my carefully composed presentation that would explain the training goals and procedures that I followed. She told me that I had to agree to move the Novitiate to Maryhill in North Dakota. I refused, unless she promised that there would be outside help in the education program. She told me there was a retired priest living at Maryhill who would teach "religion" to the novices. I knew this old priest and I had heard his tired, hackneyed sermons on several occasions. There was little of scripture in any of them. This would not be adequate in this day and age when Vatican II clearly stated in *The Basic Sixteen Documents,* page 389: "members of institutes should assiduously cultivate the spirit and practice of prayer, drawing on the authentic sources of Christian spirituality. In the first place, let them have the sacred scripture at hand daily, so that they might learn the surpassing worth of knowing Christ Jesus (Phil 3:8) by reading and meditating on the divine scriptures."

Mother Patricia disagreed and told me that she felt compelled to counsel Mother General to appoint someone else better suited to follow orders.

In misery, because of my feelings of failure, I managed to endure those days in France until we returned to Autumn Vale. There, I tearfully informed the novices of what was going to happen and that I was not to accompany them to North Dakota. They couldn't believe their ears. There were many, many days of tears and more tears. The novices, ready to take their vows, were looking forward to their new assignments after their profession in a few days. Yet, they cried for those that would come after and who would not receive the wonderful instructions that they had received from the priests of St. Basil.

Mother Ellen allowed me to present this last class to the Abbot who would accept their vows in the name of the Church. Instead of a joyous day, a blanket of gloom spread over the whole day. Right after the ceremony and banquet, I left for Wabash, Illinois where Mother Ellen had assigned me to teach in the grade school there.

Chapter 24
Moral Dilemmas
August 1966-June 1969

Only with great difficulty did I again take up my duties as an elementary classroom teacher. Completely disheartened by my failure to make any significant changes in our way of living out our commitment to the guidelines of Vatican II, life went on as before.

Many nuns, confused by the rapid changes going on in the Church, suffered serious setbacks in their spiritual life. Once a month we had to board the train to travel long hours to North Dakota for renewal meetings. These meetings aimed to unite the community in our efforts to adapt to the changes. Often times they proved to be a battleground between the very conservative members and the very liberal ones. It was hard to discern the work of the Holy Spirit in those meetings. We, who had come from great distances, after putting in a hard week at our teaching posts, found it difficult to hold on to our tempers when discussions kept going around in circles. The spirit of charity was often forgotten and those who were most outspoken for one side or the other were often the victims of vicious verbal attacks. Unfortunately, most of these tortuous discussions centered on trivial matters aimed at bringing about minimal, external changes. They took precedence over the spiritual revolution needed to bring us to a more authentic service of the Lord.

Some window-dressing changes did come about with regard to the garb. Even though the changes were gradual and minimal, not everyone accepted those changes and the battles went on.

Mother Ellen, completely at a loss about how to handle so much conflict, seemed paralyzed about what to do to keep peace in the community. Finally, she called on a Catholic psychologist from Peoria to come for monthly meetings at our convent in Wabash. Our convent seemed to be the center of the renewal movement because we spent a lot of time each month preparing for those meetings in North Dakota. It is a wonder that we ever got any teaching done with all the community meetings we were attending.

In December of 1967, Mildred's husband died of a heart attack. Millie, still suffering with bouts of depression, struggled to raise her family of nine children ranging from her oldest son of 17 to her baby daughter of 18 months.

Mother Ellen gave me permission to attend the funeral. I knew that from this time on, my sister would need all the help she could get. Her mental health had never been all that stable since her first breakdown in 1953. It pained me that I could not stay longer at this difficult time in her life.

Mother Ellen insisted that I be on hand when the meetings started with the psychologist who was to help solve our community problems. I had to hurry back to my post in Wabash. All our nuns in the area were required to attend these meetings. We discussed openly any topics causing anxiety. The psychologist was there to referee.

Before long, I became the scapegoat during many of these discussions. The conservative nuns blamed me for the trouble Mother Ellen and other superiors were experiencing in their respective areas. I tried to defend myself as best I could. The psychologist let it go on for several meetings. Then one day he asked me to stay after the others had left. I thought, *"Now what? I suppose like many others had recommended, he would admonish me to either shut up or get out."*

It turned out to be quite the contrary. In a very sympathetic manner he said, "You love your community and your superiors very much, don't you?"

My mouth dropped open and I just stared at him until it dawned on me that he, at least, recognized my true feelings. Then I began to cry. We had a very long session as he explained what was happening in my community like this:

In a science experiment, a researcher shocked rabbits in a cage with a small jolt of electricity from one direction. The rabbits got a little upset but they learned to adjust to this pattern of life. Gradually, the scientist increased in intensity those jolts and the origins came from two directions. Then they started coming from many directions without any pattern. The rabbits became frenzied, frustrated, and hostile. They even bit the hand that came in the cage with their food and water.

This psychologist said that was what was happening in the church and in some convents. Members had been able to cope when there were only a few changes that they could understand. When changes came one after another with little or no explanation, they reacted like those rabbits that were trying to hold on to their old patterns and who could not adjust to so many changes. They began to attack anyone who entered their circle of comfort.

The doctor went on to assure me that it was not my

fault. He did advise me to think about leaving this way of life if I were to retain my sanity. To me that seemed so unfair. Why should I be the one to leave? I wanted to improve community living by following the guidelines of Vatican II. I believed that those who were clinging to old outmoded ways should be the ones forced to leave. I did not like his conclusions at all but he made me promise to think about it.

Future sessions with us showed very little improvement. The same nuns continued to drag their feet at every suggestion made by the psychologist to bring about peace and harmony.

Little by little, many of us became very discouraged and there was much talk of breaking off from France because we definitely could not see eye-to-eye with them especially when it came to governing powers. Several of the younger nuns, myself included, began to meet outside the general sessions to discuss the possibilities of breaking away and starting a new community. I became very enthused about this possibility. During the Easter vacation, I even made a trip to Michigan to visit with a group of nuns who had done something similar. I did this with the permission of our house superior in Wabash.

Through the ever-active grapevine, Mother Provincial heard about this trip and she called me on the carpet at the next monthly trip to North Dakota. She sternly commanded me to stop all talk outside the general sessions. She had set up an appointment for me to receive counseling from a retired abbot whom she had invited to guide us in our renewal efforts.

I had investigated that man when he first came to our community to stay until the renewal meetings were finished. He had many weird ideas that just didn't sit right with what I had learned at Notre Dame. While arriving in Minneapolis by plane where my brother, Gene, picked me up for my home visit during the summer of 1968, I asked him if he would mind stopping at St. John's Abbey in Minnesota since I needed to consult with a priest there. I asked to see the Prior of the Abbey. He was a kindly man and easily approachable even though I had never met him before. I asked him if he knew anything about this retired Benedictine abbot. He did. He told me that this abbot had a forced retirement from an Abbey in North Dakota because his ideas of renewal did not jibe with those of Vatican II.

"Then why is he allowed to wander around North Dakota advising nuns about renewal?" I asked in astonishment.

"You have my sympathy. Be careful," were his only words of comfort.

At Maryhill, some nuns were practically worshiping at this ousted Abbot's feet, asking him to tell them exactly what to do. They believed that God was speaking through this man who was so out of touch with the guidelines of Vatican II.

Mother Ellen forced me to see him in his private quarters at Maryhill. When I entered the room, he commanded me to kneel and kiss his ring. Fat Chance! I refused because of his arrogant manners. I wanted to show him that I was no pushover whom he could easily intimidate. He became extremely abusive in his words and manner toward me. He was showing his true colors. He wanted me to quiver in fear of his authority. No way would I do that, at least not outwardly. Inwardly, there was still that legalistic struggle against the theory of absolute loyalty to a superior, "Christ's representative over you." Superiors had drilled that principle into me over the years.

Then thoroughly provoked, he threatened me: "Mother Ellen and I can have you placed in a mental institution where you will never again see the light of day."

With that, I told him in no uncertain terms that the days of the Inquisition were over and that I was not afraid of him. *Then why were my knees knocking and my voice trembling?* I knew with certainty that, though Mother Ellen did not know how to handle the strife in the community, she would never consent to such an evil act. At least, I hoped so. I left the room before I really lost my temper.

From that day, my prayers for guidance were unceasing. I did not want to leave the convent. I had been in this life now for nearly 25 years. Living back in the secular world would be a nightmare for me. I was almost 40 years old with no clue to how I would manage outside my convent walls.

This time, I was determined that I would not jump into a life-changing decision without seeking guidance from the Holy Spirit. I continued my efforts to live out my vows faithfully as I went about my daily assignments of teaching, praying, and studying ways to bring peace back to our community. I was disappointed in Mother Ellen who had promised to stand by me when she first asked me to go down this path of renewal. She had become frightened and at a loss to cope with pressures from France and from the very conservative nuns who never ceased to bend her ear. She listened and believed every bit of convent gossip that was daily growing more and more vile. Finally, one day she called me to her office and told me that I had two choices: "You can either stay silent about all matters concerning renewal or you can choose to leave."

Her ultimatum shocked me to the core. Without a word, I left her office and went to my room to let her words sink in. If I stayed, to be obedient I was destined to shrivel up and die in my spirit. I knew that I had to be faithful to what I believed had been a call from God. I was not about to leave until I was certain that He was calling me to a different area. I was not a quitter.

After many days of prayer, I sat down to write a letter to my brother, Fritz, who was living with his wife, Martha, in Atlanta, Georgia. I asked him if I could come to visit him at Easter time. He called to tell me that I was welcome to come anytime. When I arrived, I told him much of what was happening to me and of Mother Ellen's demands. After thoughtful consideration, he asked, "Isn't there some way you could try life away from the convent for a period of time before you would have to make a final decision?"

Relief swept over me when he took my plight so seriously. I responded, "Yes, there is a legal separation called exclaustration." (Literal meaning: living under one's vows outside a religious cloister with permission) He encouraged me to try that and told me I could come to live with them until I decided exactly what was right for me. I accepted his invitation with gratitude.

I asked him how he thought our mother would take the news. He answered, "She probably has known all along that you didn't belong there. Don't be afraid to tell her. She will be the one who will support you the most."

From Atlanta, I did make a quick trip home to tell my mother some of what was happening to me. True to Fritz's prophetic words she said, "I could have told you years ago, you had made a wrong choice."

Back in community, I informed the psychologist of my intention to take a sabbatical. He approved and said, "If you should decide to make that final break, please do not live with thoughts of failure. It will be of no use to think, *'If only I had been smarter, more patient, more diplomatic.'* Do not give in to any of a myriad of other regrets or guilt feelings that are likely to arise to haunt you. Just forget the past and live for the future."

Next, I wrote to Rome to obtain exclaustration papers. Rome granted them to me immediately.

Chapter 25
Plunging into the Unknown

When my local superior learned that I was leaving, she treated me with the outmost kindness. She asked a seamstress to make several outfits that I could wear after leaving the convent. When I started inquiries about locating a job, she asked a trusted woman to take me to Chicago for interviews at a national employment agency. This woman had been my friend and the parent of one of my students. She took it upon herself to secretly make an appointment for me at an Elizabeth Arden Beauty Salon. She picked me up very early in the morning so that we would have time for my beauty treatment before my appointments. This generous act of kindness touched me deeply. I had to battle against extreme shyness as they applied creams, hair treatments and arched my eyebrows. Their treatments did wonders for my morale. My interviews went well even though I was a nervous wreck. However, when they did a job search in the Atlanta area where I intended to live, they found no immediate job openings that matched my qualifications.

Finally, the day came for me to leave the convent. My heart cried at leaving the life I had finally accepted after so many years of questioning and doubt. Many of my friends had abandoned me and no great numbers came to see me off. For sure, they gave me no grand farewell party; they may have simply drawn a great collective sigh of relief to be rid of the maverick that went about too aggressively trying to make changes in the community. I flew to Atlanta with the $600 the community gave me to tide me over until I found a job. I thought this was very generous. I had no idea how fast that sum of money would vanish.

Martha and Fritz welcomed me and did everything in their power to ease me into a world that was foreign in so many respects. The apartment complex in which Fritz and Martha lived surrounded a large community swimming pool. Martha urged me to get out in the sun to dispose of my convent pallor. I had wanted to remain completely anonymous but she organized pool parties and introduced me to every tenant as a "nun on leave." Of course, as far as I was concerned that went over like a big, wet blanket. People tended to clam up or they fussed by trying to show me deference: giving up their chairs or making excuses if some vulgar words were expressed in my presence.

Martha meant well but I wanted no special treatment. Further, I did not like to answer a bunch of silly curiosity questions about why I was working outside of the convent. The tenants were not all that eager to have the equivalent of what they perceived as a "hall monitor" at their parties.

Martha welcomed everyone into her home, the ultimate "hostess with the mostest." Their home was like a thoroughfare where people came in, sat down in the small kitchen, drank some free booze, and popped out again at anytime during the evening hours. The apartment quickly became smoke-filled even though visitors and relatives often came with their children and anyone else who happened to cross their path. They came in from the highways and byways. Anytime was "Party Time" in this household. They turned no one away. This style of life was a real shock to me. The evening meal sometimes came well after midnight. Martha was adept in her attempts to introduce me to a lifestyle without rigid schedules. I often wanted to retreat to my bedroom to enjoy some moments of peace and quiet. There was not a chance of that happening. Martha came knocking on the door, asking me to come out and be sociable. If I dared look at the clock, she would invariably ask, "Are you on some kind of medication that you need to watch the time?"

Each day I scoured the want ads to find a summer job and, at the same time, I looked for a school that would hire me for the upcoming school term. In the meantime, my brother helped me look for an inexpensive car so that when I landed a job, I would have a way to get to it.

He gave advice in this matter and in many other things where I waffled uneasily about making necessary decisions. But when it came down to the final moment, I was on my own. He refused to be an enabler who kept me from maturing in this world. Martha was great in that respect also. She took me shopping for appropriate clothes. But shy as I was about that, I had to make the final choices.

As my money began to run low, I grasped at any job. I answered an ad looking for a person to sell cosmetics. I was that desperate. I learned to sell cosmetics for a company that demonstrated their products at home parties. I learned the tricks of putting on makeup and of salesmanship from the boss lady, a talented cosmetologist, who could have sold her products to the most prudish Mother Superior. My mentor was cutthroat in her determination to sell to every woman whether they could afford it or not. I did make good money but I refused to follow her philosophy. If a perspective customer flat out said "No," that was good enough for me. I went on to those who were interested.

Finally, I found a job teaching speed-reading to students at an accelerated learning summer school. It was located at the opposite end of Atlanta. I needed to use the freeway to reach that location. I asked Fritz to go with me the first time but he insisted that I could find my way. I did and was later happy that he encouraged me to venture out on my own.

With each day, it became a little easier to adjust. I began to relax, especially when I received a call for an interview for a teaching job for the next school year. This school was in the poorest county of the state and the poorest school in that county located about 25 miles from Atlanta.

This school hired me, as well as the wife of one of Fritz's co-workers, Grace Johnson, so we planned to take turns driving to our job. We, (Grace J. and Grace E. as we came to be known) were the first "outsiders" hired by the school. In the past, they hired someone from the community who might or might not have been fully qualified. Most of the people of this community were Baptists who were a little suspicious of persons from another denomination. During the first days of orientation, one teacher whispered to me, "I hear there is a Catholic on the faculty."

Grace J., who was neither Catholic nor Baptist, overheard the conversation. She frantically gave me signs that cautioned me not to reveal that I was that person. I asked the teacher, "Does that make a big difference to you?"

"Why, yes," she responded. "Catholics are trying to take over the world. We don't want them teaching our children."

In reply, I said, "I have never heard that about Catholics before. I don't think that it will happen any time soon." I did not like remaining silent about my faith but for the time being, I heeded my friend's hint that it was best to let them get to know me first before putting up walls of division. If they found out that I was not only Catholic but also a nun, they might want me tarred and feathered.

I missed teaching my students about Jesus. Teaching in a public school, I assumed that I must not attempt to bring God into the classroom. One day I asked one of the most veteran teachers if she ever read the Bible to the children in her class. She answered, "Of course; not only can you do it, the parents expect you to do it and to start the day with the Lord's Prayer."

That really surprised me. I began that practice right away. Those children were the most attentive and reverent students I had ever seen as I read a passage or two from the Bible each day. Their demeanor was plainly reverent. I was impressed. When we stood for prayer, I never had to scold anyone for looking around or for not paying attention. These children may not have had the best schooling but it was easy to tell they had received a very deep Christian education at home.

The principal hired me to teach the fifth and sixth grades. I was stunned to learn in the first days that most of my students could read only short common words like "but, the, and go." They were good in math but that was about all. Until they learned to read better, I had to read aloud their history, geography, science and English lessons. I noticed that they watched me very closely, really looking intently at me all the while I read. They never tried to follow along in their own texts. These students kept their eyes glued on me. I had never had students that paid that close attention. It was almost like they were deaf and were lip reading. Finally, one day I asked them why they kept staring at me. One little girl with neatly braided blond hair and a face splashed with abundant freckles, raised her hand as she explained in her lazy Southern drawl, "Why, Miss

Feltis, we just "l o v e" to listen to your Yankee talk." I told them that I enjoyed their quaint southern expressions too. It took me awhile to understand that they only wanted to open a window when they asked permission to "crack a winda." When they said they were having "hushpuppies" for lunch, I learned that they did not intend to munch on their shoes.

At least my accent kept their attention, but I had to find a way to entice them to want to read for themselves. My companion, Grace J., knew of a school in Atlanta that was discarding some old readers. She took me there and we came away with books from the primary grades and up.

I asked my students, "Do you want to learn to read?" Every hand went up. "We will have to start at the very beginning. Are you sure that reading first grade books will not make you feel sad?"

"No! We want to learn how to read. Nobody has ever taught us how."

I was cautious about handing them primers but they responded enthusiastically to my every attempt to help them learn. They willingly stayed in at midmorning recess and at noon to learn more quickly. By Christmas vacation, they had advanced several grades.

They were so unspoiled. I issued fake money to them for every word they learned to read, spell and write correctly. On Friday afternoon, instead of our usual classes, I held an auction for small items that they could buy with their accumulated wealth. They treasured everything they bought as if it were a precious trophy proclaiming their successes. Everyone had a chance to buy something. Every Friday morning they rushed to meet the car as we drove up to the school. They clamored to carry my briefcase as if even that was a reward for their courageous efforts. I never heard any youngster say, "I don't like this thing." They were happy with every little item I bought for them.

Among the teachers, one other "outsider" joined the faculty a little late in the first quarter. This man, Mr.

Macho, had been in the military. Rumor had it that he had a steel plate in his head. In my estimation that was about all that he carried in his head; his actions portrayed a blustering, self-doubting bully. He taught the eighth graders. He always carried a big wooden "board of education" with him when his class came out of their room for any reason. He often struck the rear end of a student who may have stepped out of line.

No teacher ever took him to task for it. He hardly ever spoke a word to any of us, his fellow teachers, until I asked him, "Why do you have to resort to violence with these children who are so polite and well behaved?"

"They need to know that I am the boss around here," he replied.

"You must be very insecure," I replied.

He just snorted in contempt at that remark.

Soon after school started, our good and gentle principal, Mr. Gordon, died unexpectedly. The whole grief-stricken community held a memorial in the gym one evening. All the teachers, students and their parents were present. Right in the middle of that prayerful meeting, Mr. Macho took center stage and began to address the parents, "If you choose to make me principal, I will bring order to this school. You parents don't know how to discipline your children. I will do it for you."

On and on he ranted and raved about his qualifications and then suddenly he began to read a long poem, *Gunga Din,* by Rudyard Kipling. It is a story about a native water-bearer who saves a British soldier's life.

The audience was shocked as Mr. Macho waved his arms about, knelt on one knee, and shouted out this complex poem in a most histrionic and inappropriate manner. Grace J. and I looked at each other after the first couple of lines had been yelled out. Reading each other's thoughts, we both got up at the same time and left the building. Some brave parents followed suit but most sat in stupefied silence. They had no idea what this poem had to do with paying tribute to their deceased principal.

The next morning in the teacher's lounge, Mr. Macho deigned to talk to me. "What did you think of my tribute last night?" (He had been so wrapped up in himself, he had not seen us leave the gym.)

"I thought you were the best personification of a horse's patoot that I have ever seen. You should be ashamed of yourself for talking down to the good people of this community," was my reply.

He was stunned by my remarks and several of the teachers present began to smile as they saw the deflated expression on his face.

Throughout the day, teachers came knocking on my classroom door to tell me how much they appreciated my support of them in the face of that obnoxious teacher. Grace J. and I went home that night feeling we had personally experienced the same joy that David felt when he had vanquished Goliath.

Needless to say, Mr. Macho was not chosen as a replacement for the deceased principal. Compared to Mr. Gordon, Mr. Macho could repeat with head hung low, the last few lines of the poem *Gunga Din*: "Though I've belted you and flayed you, By the livin' Gawd that made you, You're a better man than I am, Gunga Din."

Chapter 26
New Challenges

At times, I still felt like I had dropped down from a far-off planet, an alien in this world. About the time I was beginning to get a grip in adjusting, a new test arose.

Just before our Christmas vacation started, my oldest brother, Paul, called to tell us that Mildred was again in the hospital because she could not cope with all her problems. Paul had been there in Osceola, Wisconsin to help her as much as he could. He asked me to come to help during my upcoming holiday vacation.

Although I had been looking forward to my first Christmas without all the snow, cold and blizzards of the Midwest, I knew that I wanted to help with the children who would also be into vacation and would, therefore, be at loose ends without their mother. As a further incentive, Fritz promised me, "The weather will be invigorating."

You better believe it was.

It was difficult for me to know just what to do in that busy household once I arrived in Wisconsin. I could easily handle forty children in a classroom but it was not as easy to keep a family of nine going without parents there to love and guide them. It had been a year since they had lost their father to a fatal heart attack.

Besides trying to fill in as a substitute mother for their emotional needs, I needed help in meeting their hunger at mealtime. I was not a skilled cook by a long shot. Beverly, age 10, patiently demonstrated the proper way to make oatmeal so that it didn't come out all lumpy. She thought it hilarious that I was so ignorant about such common ordinary things. Janine, age 12, taught me a thing or two about cooking some of their other favorite foods. There was no money to take them out to a restaurant or a fast-food place. I was grateful that they were not picky eaters. They ate the plain fare I put on the table without complaints. It was easy to see that my nieces and nephews had lived in a loving atmosphere despite their early loss of their father and their mother's ill health.

Little Monica had to be potty trained. I had no clue about the correct way to do this. When I thought it was about time for her to pee, I would sit her on the pot and tell her to stay there until she tinkled. She did not like this one bit. All the older brother and sisters would glare at me for being so mean to their little sister. This darling three-year-old looked up at me from her uncomfortable throne and told me in no uncertain terms, "Get on the plane, go home and don't come back!"

The others echoed that refrain in their minds, I am sure, but they were too polite to tell me off like Monica had just done. I was in my strictest teacher mode most of the time. Finally, one day after I had humiliated Tim and Ron by going to the school gym to drag them back to the house for some chore, Ron said in disgust, "We don't need a bossy school teacher around here. We need our mother."

192

With what I meant as sympathy I replied, "I know but since your mother is sick, you need to help me with all the chores. Surely you can understand that, can't you?"

Looking back on it later, I realized that it probably would have been better for them to have a little fun than for me to be constantly trying to make everything perfect. I showed my own immaturity at handling the problems that arose in this situation. I wondered how Mildred had coped as long as she had. The children were exceptionally good but their care required a lot of energy.

Each day I came up with a list of chores for each one. They worked diligently for the most part even while they grumbled about me being the worst slave driver they had ever seen.

On Saturday, the older children pleaded with me to let them go to church for a service. At first, I thought they were just making an excuse to get out of work. When Janine assured me there really was something going on in church that they were supposed to attend, I let them go. They rushed out of the house like chickens released after being cooped up after a long winter.

During the service, David fainted. Surrounded by concerned parishioners when he regained consciousness, David moaned, "Aunt Grace made me work too hard!"

On their return to the house, they were laughing about the incident so hard, they could hardly tell me what had happened. As they told me about David's confession to the whole parish, I decided that I needed to ease up a bit.

My mom called often to learn how things were going. Even little Monica wanted to talk to her grandma. When it was Monica's turn to talk, she said, "Grandma, do you want to hear a poem I learned?"

Of course, Grandma was delighted to listen. Monica proceeded in her very best dramatic voice: "Teacher, teacher, I declare. Someone stole my underwear. Is it pink or is it blue? Oh! My gosh! It's number two!"

Hardly able to contain her laughter, Grandma said, "Now, who taught you that poem?"

With her most impish grin she replied, "Aunt Grace did."

I think she got her revenge on me for the potty training. I had never heard that poem before. Honest!

Every day I coaxed the little ones to dress in their snowsuits, mittens, caps and boots to play outdoors. They wanted me to play with them like their mom always did but I begged off as I needed a little time to rest. Fritz called often to check on how I was holding up. When I told him that I was usually exhausted at the end of the day, he said, "Why don't you try smoking a cigarette just to relax?"

I had not smoked a cigarette since my childhood experiments, but I bought a pack to give it a try. After lighting up the first one and inhaling my first drag, I coughed until my eyes watered, but I kept trying. Before long, I was thoroughly addicted. *Thanks Fritz!*

Doctors had diagnosed Mildred as having pernicious anemia, which was a contributing factor to her chronic fatigue, habitual weakness and long periods of severe depression. I didn't fully realize that her sickness had put a long-term strain on the family.

In the past, Janine had taken on many of the tasks that normally fell to a mother. She tried to keep order when Mildred slept for much of the day when she was at her lowest. But the younger ones grew tired of assigned tasks from Janine that deprived them of their normal playtime. They often resented her role as their replacement mother.

For the most part, the children were easily entertained. They loved to play cards and board games. The older ones often seemed to brood and they found an escape by sitting for long periods watching TV as if it would offer a solution to their inability to understand what was happening to their family.

Just before New Year's Day, Mildred came home for a

short visit. She was delighted to see her children, as they were to see her. On New Year's Eve, she decided she want to celebrate with some of her friends and me. We coaxed the older children to be in charge of the younger ones and we barhopped all evening. Now that was still a rather daunting new experience for me, but Mildred seemed to enjoy it. She danced, laughed, and seemed to forget she had to go back to the hospital for further treatment.

When the time came for her to go back to the hospital, she asked me to come to live with her permanently. I didn't know how to react to that request; I knew that she definitely needed help. I was tired at the end of each day yet I was in good health and I didn't want to leave her alone.

After praying about what to do, I decided to go to the public school in Osceola to see if I could get a job teaching there during the second semester. The principal said that there was an opening in the elementary level. First, my Georgia principal had to release me from my contract there. I needed to go back to settle things. Mildred assured me that she would be able to cope until I returned to help her.

I flew back to Atlanta where I contacted my principal who said he could release me only at the end of January. I called Mil to tell her that I would be there in early February. The school in Osceola consented to hold the job for me by hiring subs until I arrived. The principal and Mildred's sons were good friends. Maybe this helped in securing my job.

Fritz was worried about all of this. He brooded about it for several days and finally told me that I had better call her doctor in Milwaukee to see if my moving in with Mil was the prudent thing to do.

When I called, her doctor told me that I would be making a big mistake if I did as I was proposing. "Mildred is making great progress. If you come to live with her, she will pass on all of her responsibilities to you. You will then usurp her place as mother, and you will have ten children to care for instead of nine."

I was afraid these words would crush Mil's spirit. I asked the doctor exactly how I should break this news to her. The doctor's advice was that I should always tell her the truth. She told me exactly what to say, "Your doctor has advised against it because she thinks you are getting stronger and she believes that you can handle your problems on your own."

It was with great trepidation that I finally called Mil on Feb. 13. It just didn't seem right to leave her alone. I can still hear her voice when I told her I couldn't come and why. She answered very calmly, "That's okay, Grace, I never should have asked you in the first place."

There was something not right about her voice. I knew that she was not taking that news very well. This truly alarmed me, but I didn't know what else to do. I told her that I would call her often and that we could talk about summer plans. She agreed that would be a good idea.

The next day, Fritz got the shocking call that Mildred had taken her life. We were devastated and concerned about the effect this would have on the children, already wounded by the loss of their father and the prolonged illness of their mother. Almost immediately, my mother called me because she was concerned that I might feel guilty about my decision to follow the doctor's recommendation to leave Mildred face her problems alone. That was the least of my fears. What was foremost in my mind was the well being of the children.

After her husband's death, Mildred had named Fritz legal guardian should anything happen to her. We traveled by car to Osceola for the funeral. After we laid Mildred to rest, Fritz called a family meeting. An aunt on the father's side from the state of Washington was present also. She asked if she could take care of the younger children. She offered to take them to her home. We thought this was a miracle from heaven. She and her husband seemed like the ideal people to care for these orphaned children. The older boys and Janine had lined up boldly, insisting that their brothers and sisters remain together. After much discussion, Fritz finally consented and helped the paternal aunt obtain all the information, school and health records needed to make the transition for the children as painless as possible. Tim and Ron stayed behind to finish their schooling. We returned to Atlanta believing that our nieces and nephews were in good hands. We were to find out later that was indeed not the case.

One of the biggest mistakes in all of these processes and decisions was our ignorance of the total impact that all these past tragedies and losses had made on the minds and hearts of the children of this family. In that day and age, there were no school or general counseling sessions offered to help hurting people grapple with life's tragedies. The children had to figure out on their own the reasons for their losses. No doubt, some of them began to blame themselves for what had happened. Others may have blamed God, the church, their neighbors, or family members. They needed daily assurance that they were not to blame, that there is no clear answer to how and why sickness can distort a good person's thinking to such a degree that they are no longer capable of making rational decisions.

There was never a moment when any of Mildred's parents, brothers or sisters ever thought that she was not welcomed into her loving God's arms at the moment of her death. We had known her from the beginning; she was always so loving, conscientious, and devoted to God. Her sickness did not cancel what she held deep in her own heart of hearts. She was always a child of God, completely loved by him and embraced in his tenderness. To believe otherwise would result in useless torment. She is in heaven with all of God's family, looking on us now with a spirit that is free forever from the effects of sickness and death.

197

We can all look forward to the day when we can be with her again to enjoy our time in eternity praising God for his wonderful mercy and kindness. She can now help us in more ways than she could while bound on earth by the limitations of her human existence.

Chapter 27
At Peace

Sometime earlier in that year, I had written to Rome for a dispensation from my vows. In it, I had to explain my reasons for leaving the convent. It all boiled down to following my conscience. Vatican II made it perfectly clear that every individual has the right to follow his or her conscience as long as it is an informed conscience. I certainly had prayed and sought right counsel to a greater degree before making this decision than I had done before entering the convent in the first place. Rome granted me my exemption in record time.

I knew that I would never go back to convent life again unless the Holy Spirit literally kicked me through a convent door. I did not regret the years I had spent in the service of the Lord. I was grateful for the education that I had received, for the love of prayer that God had fostered in me, and for the growth of my desire to be at one with my

Lord and Savior. Now, I needed to discern where the Lord wanted me to serve him in a new way. I had to seek my growth in spirituality arising from interior convictions rather than from external sources. I realized that what I do is not as important as why and how I act in any situation. I still had to struggle with feeling that I should have tried harder to compromise instead of being so adamant about bringing about immediate changes. At other times, I knew that it is futile to second-guess what might have been.

After being away from the convent for all this time, I woke up one morning and realized that my migraine headaches had disappeared. I was amazed. I began to believe that this was all part of God's plan for me. Like my mother always said, "Divine Providence assures us that we can walk in peace by doing his will." I was at peace at last. Even though I still encounter people who openly show disapproval of me because I left the convent, I have not let their judgment take away my peace. I had followed my conscience and no one has the right to judge my relationship with my God. It doesn't feel good to feel their scrutiny but I choose not to let it throw me into peace-stealing turmoil.

Fritz and Martha encouraged me to start dating. I was busy with my schoolwork and with adjusting to secular life. I had not taken time to think about men, not that I hadn't noticed them. Even in the convent, I always enjoyed their company and they never intimidated me. I had always preferred their conversations and dealings to those of most women. I suppose that came from having five brothers.

A remarkably handsome man by the name of Leonard moved into an apartment just above us. Martha quickly introduced herself to him, welcomed him as she did every person she met, and soon he was dropping in to share free drinks with Fritz and Martha in the evening after work. Fritz soon discerned that many of his stories contained many inconsistencies. Leonard claimed he was an administrator at a large Atlanta firm. He had a smooth lingo and a charming manner and smile. I was shy and stayed in my room correcting papers, preparing lessons or trying to maintain my prayer life, whenever he was around. Martha tried to persuade me to join them but I always found an excuse to stay out of sight as much as possible.

On one such evening, one of my friends came to visit me. Finola McGuire, a woman of about my age, had befriended me when I joined Christ the King parish. She was a petite, vivacious, Irish redhead. As we were talking, Leonard passed by the window on the way to his apartment. Finola immediately ogled over his good looks and tasteful attire. She begged me to take her to his apartment to meet him. I did not want to do that at all, but she was very insistent. I finally gave in. We went up to his door and I timidly knocked, not knowing exactly what I was going to say if he answered the door; I was secretly hoping he would not respond. However, he answered and showed no amazement when he saw the two of us waiting there. He politely invited us in and I introduced Finola. He gave her his full attention. Soon they were laughing and joking as though they had known each other for years. I sat quietly joining in, if and when, I thought it was appropriate. When it came time to leave, Finola lingered, hoping Leonard would ask her for a date, but he did not. He thanked us for our visit and that was that.

The next morning as I came out to leave for school, Leonard was leaning against my car. I wondered what in the world he was doing. He asked me why I had brought Finola to meet him. I stammered that she was hoping to strike up a friendship with him. He told me he was not interested in a friendship with her but that he would like to take me out to dinner some evening if that was agreeable. I told him that I really was not into dating but that I would think about it. When I asked Fritz about going out with Leonard, he encouraged me to accept his invitation. I was extremely nervous. I bought a new dress, had my hair and nails done and went off with him to a wonderful restaurant for an evening meal.

Indeed, Leonard was a smooth talker. I didn't have to struggle to make conversation. He carried the ball all through supper, mostly talking about his life experiences. At one time, he said that he came from New York. Later he referred to his home in Chicago. Then he said he was an ousted Bishop from Louisiana. Still later, he told of his life as a Trappist monk in Missouri. My conclusion by the end of the evening was that he was a compulsive liar that I wouldn't trust very far. Still I enjoyed his company but I knew that I would have to be on my guard. He knew from Martha that I had been a nun so maybe he thought he would impress me with his outlandish stories. For all I cared, Finola could have him.

Nevertheless, he pursued me and I went out with him a few more times until he suggested sharing his bed. That ended that. I did date a few more men that Fritz brought home from his company, but nothing very serious ever developed from any of them. Fiona and I went to the local bars on occasion and we did have some good times, dancing and drinking with whomever we met there. Naïve as I was, it is a miracle that I didn't get into real trouble. In those days, there were still many good people just out for a good time. We met no one who stalked or sulked around, looking to ravish us.

There was a family in the complex that had come here from Columbia, South America. Martha struck up a friendship with them, as was her wont. A wealthy aunt, Rosealba, came to visit them from their homeland. She loved to shop but she was having a difficult time finding anyone who had the time to accompany her on her prolonged shopping sprees. Martha, with her heart full of charity, volunteered my services to her without consulting me.

Many days I arrived home from school, tired and looking forward to relaxing before correcting my papers or preparing for the next day of school. Martha met me at the door and informed me that Rosealba was waiting for me to drive her to the some exclusive dress shop or shopping mall. I was not always gracious about complying with Martha's wishes but I would give in because Martha had done so much for me. Off Rosealba and I went. On reaching the shop, I found a place to rest and Rosealba tried on clothes or shopped for an hour or two. I didn't exactly pout but I was definitely not the picture of a cheerful giver either. In later years, Rosealba, treated me with supreme generosity when she invited me to stay in her home in South America over a Christmas vacation.

Earlier in the year, I had seen an ad in a paper that asked for teachers in many different places away from the United States. I went for an interview hoping that I would find a teaching job far away where I could learn what it was truly like to live as a person in my own right. I applied for teaching jobs in Alaska, Australia, Greenland among many other remote areas. It took a full year for any school to answer any of my numerous applications.

Finally, I received a call from Mr. Branick, the principal of a school in Venezuela, South America. He wanted to interview me for a job in a school for the children of big business concerns located in a city called Valencia, Venezuela. We agreed to meet at the Atlanta airport on a certain day he arrived from Venezuela. I was very nervous and excited about the prospect of teaching outside of the United States where I could be myself with no one else around who knew that I had spent more than half my life in a convent.

Mr. Branick approached me at the information counter as we had prearranged. He inquired about my previous experience and I plied him with questions about how he ran the school. He intently looked over my resume. Somewhat timidly he asked, "How is it that you taught in so many Catholic schools? As much as I hated to divulge any information about my time in the convent, I made a quick decision to tell him that I had been a nun. I was afraid that would turn him off. Quite the contrary, he was pleased. He was a Catholic. He said that he was looking for teachers who would be willing to stay more than one year. He was even more pleased to learn there was no man in my life when he flat out asked me about it. He felt there was a better chance that I would remain for several years if I were unfettered in my personal relationships. After an hour or so, he said, "You're hired! Do you accept the terms of my contract?" I signed on the dotted line and went out of that airport riding on Cloud Nine. I was eager to begin preparing everything so that I could leave in the autumn of 1970.

I had lost some weight during those last three hectic years in the convent, but I was still too heavy. I enrolled in a health club and went there faithfully almost every day. I exercised and swam in the huge pool. After returning from my classes every Friday, I finished my exercises with a wonderful massage from a big lady who pounded every muscle into mush. I began to feel like a new person who could again smile easily and often.

By the end of the summer, I expected to leave for South America but there was much political unrest in Venezuela at that time. It took several months for that country to accept my visa. Fritz had helped me ready my trunk for shipping and I had my passport in hand. I became more and more frustrated as each day passed.

In the meantime, Fritz received frantic letters from Janine, written from Washington where she and the six younger members of the family had moved. Janine reported that she and the other children were unhappy because of unfair treatment by their aunt who had taken them into her home. With each letter that she wrote, she became more and more insistent that he must rescue them from this home where they were not welcome.

Since I was the only one waiting around to go to my job, Fritz asked me to fly to Washington to see for myself if there was any truth to Janine's pleas for help. We both realized that the children would have trouble adjusting to their new home with neither of their parents nor their two older brothers to help them. Still, it was now late August. It had been six months since Mildred had died. We had hoped that they would have adjusted by now. None of us were really attuned to the need for counseling when tragedy struck a family. In later years, we would learn that such shocks as these children had experienced had far-reaching effects. Children have been known to blame themselves, others in the family or the doctor who had treated Mildred. No one had taken them aside to let them express their sorrow, their loss, nor to answer their questions about what had happened to their mother. I have asked God to forgive us our ignorance and insensitivity to their grief.

Their new foster mother and father did not want me to come. They said that I would disrupt the children's adjustment. Nevertheless, Fritz could not just ignore Janine. I flew to Redding, Washington and stayed with Rose, a sister of Martha, who lived near the children's home.

When I arrived, I called their home to tell them I wanted to see my nieces and nephews. Even little Monica, who had once told me to "Go away and never come back!" welcomed me with open arms. The fact that I bore some resemblance to their mother may have prompted their spontaneous joy at seeing me, yet I sensed it was more than that.

I found the house very crowded. All seven of the children lived in the basement with little space to accommodate them. Since the children could not freely talk in the house, I suggested that we go for a walk. The children poured out their tales of woe to me. They told of discrimination in the way their aunt treated them in comparison to the four children of their own family. They claimed the aunt often sent them to the basement when she made cookies or other goodies that she did not want to share with them. She was not a Catholic and she forced them to pray with her in a fashion that was not familiar to them. She constantly spoke ill of their deceased mother. That really hit a very sore spot with them.

When my visit concluded, I called Fritz to tell him that Janine was not lying about the basics of their care. I believed that the ultimate reason these parents took in these children was because of the money that came to them from the Social Security funds available to the children. Now it would be Fritz' responsibility to decide what to do because Mildred had asked him to be the children's advocate in case of her demise.

Chapter 28
Another Awakening August –
October 1970

After leaving Washington and my unhappy nieces and nephews, I flew back to North Dakota to visit with my parents before returning to Atlanta to await the call from South America. My parents had not seen me since I had left the convent because I had gone directly to Atlanta from Wabash, Illinois.

It was an absolute joy to be home for more than just one day. Mom and I had many long talks while dad was bringing in the harvest from his beloved fields. She was totally supportive of my decision to leave the convent. She warned me that some people might criticize me for not living out my vows. She urged me to be strong and stand firm in what I believed. She especially prayed that I would not keep any feelings of bitterness in my heart for those who had wronged me. We discussed the loss of Mildred in our lives. She had worried that I had blamed myself because I had not gone to help when Mildred had asked. I assured her that I had worked through all of those guilty thoughts that had tried to steal my peace. I knew with certainty that I had followed the counsel of the doctor who was supposed to know Mildred's mental state better than I did. She had told me that Mildred would make it on her own. It would have been pure arrogance on my part to ignore her advice.

On one of those late summer days while I was at home, Rosemary, Gene's wife, invited me to supper at their home in Lisbon. When I arrived, Rosemary was outside, sitting at a picnic table, peeling potatoes. She carefully lined layers of potatoes, onions, and ham in a large roaster. As she continued her preparations, we chatted all the while.

Gene was home on vacation from his government employment in the Pacific Islands. At this moment, he was trying to persuade the youngest children, Barbara, Mike, and Roberta to help him mow and clean up the lawn. He stopped occasionally from his work to exchange a few words with us. Whenever he did, his reluctant helpers tried to make their escape. The very youngest, Maria, played happily under the shade of the trees. She was the only one who actually wanted to be included in the work force. As hard as she tried, her four-year-old muscles could not remove very many weeds.

Suddenly, Rosemary announced that we needed to make a trip to the bar, as the beer supply was getting low. She put her roaster of food in the oven, advised her husband to watch the children, and off we went to get a fresh supply.

The saloon, located on the extreme southern edge of the town, flashed a neon sign, "Last Chance Bar." Since it was well after working hours, there were many customers seated in booths and on bar stools. We managed to find a booth and Rosemary ordered a beer for each of us. Then she noticed a nice looking man seated on one of the stools near us. She called to him, "Hey, Dick, come on over and see who is with me."

Immediately, I recognized him as my childhood sweetheart, Dick Taylor. When Rosemary asked him to try to identify me, he said that he was sure I was a Feltis girl, but he was at a loss to know which one. He reasoned, "Mary and Lil have red hair. Mildred is deceased." With a marvelous smile, he added, " If this is Aggie she sure has aged well."

Since I had been away for so many years, my name never entered his mind, as he later told me. Rosemary laughed and introduced me, inviting Dick to join us. We hung out there for a little while until Rosemary asked Dick to join us for supper. He readily accepted. He and I had several opportunities to be alone during the evening. We recalled many memories of our elementary school days. Before the evening was over, Dick asked if I would be interested in going out with him some evening. I agreed, but I let him know that I would be leaving for Atlanta in about six days. Maybe my stop at the Last Chance Bar would prove to be the beginning of something new and wonderful in my life.

The next day Dick called to set up a date. We agreed that there was nothing to prevent us from having supper together that very evening. Arriving slightly inebriated, though minimally detectable, he picked me up at my parents' home and we went to the Oakes Supper Club. He apologized for his indulgence in a few beers before coming. He said that he needed a drink to bolster up his courage. This proved to be the first evening of a whirlwind courtship.

Earlier in the day, I had received a call from Fritz telling me that the South America principal expected me to be in Venezuela in ten days. Dick and I had five evenings left to enjoy each other's company. We went out every evening. We bantered easily over our dinners together. We touched on many subjects, including our convictions about religion and morality. He quickly discovered many things that had happened in his life had no similar counterpart in mine. His father died when Dick was only months old, his mother had never remarried and had died in 1958. He was sent to Japan during the Korean conflict. I was quite clueless in many areas that were quite commonplace to him. He knew all about cars and how they worked, how to manage his own finances, and to deal with the public when it was necessary. He knew nothing about convent life or what it had been like for me. These discrepancies in our lives were often the occasion for playful teasing on Dick's part. It was difficult for him to realize what a sheltered life I had lived.

There never seemed to be enough time to catch up on all the times that we had been apart. Almost imperceptibly, amid a great deal of confusion about their proper place, I began to experience and warily to enjoy strong, unfamiliar and wonderfully mysterious sexual feelings. I had learned to repress these feelings through the years. Since I had entered the convent so very young, any strong sexual urges that I had experienced, I learned to squelch very quickly. Our training did not allow us to even admit that sexuality was a normal part of life. Now these erotic feelings were suddenly, strange, wonderful, exciting and yet very disturbing. I wanted to pursue them but my convent training told me that I had to hold back such "unholy" feelings. Dick seemed to be fully aware of the strong attraction that was building up between us but he was very considerate of my obvious moral dilemmas. He was the perfect gentleman. In spite of my confusion and embarrassment, which he easily dispelled, he slowly earned my trust and love. At that time in history, I had never heard anything about safe sex or birth control pills. With Dick, so

210

far, I had no need for it. Thankfully, he had enough self-discipline for the both of us.

When I had known Dick in grade school and during those few days we spent together on my visits home from boarding school, he was just beginning to mature into a gentle, caring and compassionate person. Now he had matured. He was very handsome, tanned, tall and slim. He kept his hair, which had turned prematurely gray at 25, neatly trimmed in a crew cut. There had always been areas of his personality that even he did not understand. His need for alcohol to get him through those places would later become evident even to my naïve discernment. However, during our first dates, we were both on our best behavior. We both enjoyed drinks with our dinners but we were careful not to consume enough to lose our sense of balance.

Dick had cared for his mother and his Aunt Edith until they died. He told me that he was often very lonely. He was very shy at first but soon he was telling me all about his experiences in Japan during the Korean War era and about his family, his friends and his work. I told him a little about my life as a teacher. He didn't seem to mind that I had been a nun. He was nominally a Lutheran but he had not been attending church regularly since his mother had died in 1957. I was one month and two days older than he. We would both turn 41 in the fall.

On Sunday, he took me to Grand Rapids Park where his sister, LuWanna, hosted a large family picnic. He introduced me to each of them, and I could tell they were very surprised to learn that I was back in circulation. We had a great time. Later that evening when we were alone, he opened up about the women he had dated in the past. I found myself filled with unexpected jealousy. He admitted that while he was in the service and after, he had experienced several serious relationships and a few short-term affairs. He claimed he had never found any woman with whom he wanted to spend the rest of his life. Out of the blue, as he retrieved a little velvet box from his pocket, he asked me to marry him. I looked in amazement at the beautiful diamond ring that he was holding in his hand. He explained that he had gone to the jeweler in Lisbon on Saturday and had purchased this engagement ring with the hope that I would accept his proposal.

In my heart I was quite sure that I wanted to marry him yet I knew that I needed time to find out how I was going to cope in this unfamiliar world. I was still a virgin both physically and emotionally. He was a little disappointed to learn that I needed to honor the contract that I had signed to teach in Venezuela. He begged me to try to find some loophole so that I wouldn't need to go so far away. I assured him that if our feelings for each other were real, a year apart would not be fatal to our relationship. I also knew that Mr. Branick would be very disappointed to learn of this development.

At first, my mother was alarmed when I told her of Dick's proposal. Dick had, at one time, briefly dated Mildred. She told me there had been a couple of occasions when she thought that Dick had consumed too many beers to take Mil out on a date. I agreed that Dick did like his beer, but I didn't believe it would be a big problem. Only on our first date, I did notice his overindulgence. Typically, I dismissed my mother's worries, confident that we would cross that bridge if it became more serious.

On Monday, Dick took me to Fargo to catch the plane back to Atlanta. Sadness filled our hearts when we had to leave each other so soon. He asked me to wear his ring while I was away even though I had not yet fully committed to him. I consented as long as he accepted that it did not mean something absolutely binding on either of us. I could see that Dick, who had respectfully and guardedly awakened my long-dormant passions, was necessarily concerned that I would have trouble keeping those passions in check if I met men who would not hesitate to take advantage of my vulnerability. That ring did much to boost my morale in the days to come, and it helped ward off unwanted attention from the some of the amorous males I would come to meet in South America. I was to learn also that it would mean nothing to others far less scrupulous than Dick.

When I arrived back in Atlanta, I had to scurry to get all in order to leave. Fritz and Martha were great in their continued solicitude for me. They fully approved of my involvement with Dick whom Fritz had known for many years. With so much gratitude for all they had done for me, I told Fritz that I just didn't know how I could ever repay them for their goodness. In all good humor, Fritz replied, "Try cash!" All the money in the world would not have come close to matching their generosity toward me.

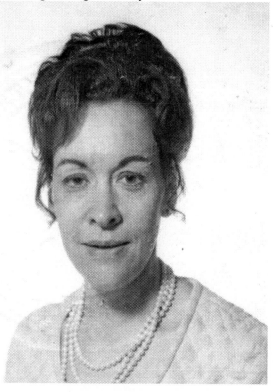

As soon as I got my belongings ready, I was off to a new adventure in Venezuela. I needed time to get my bearings and to find out how the people of this country would treat me as a layperson. As I boarded the plane, I recalled the last poignant moments of my leaving my first love, Dick, behind in North Dakota. We had called each other every day since then. It had been very difficult for me to say goodbye but I knew that it was even harder for Dick. I was going to a new land and new experiences that would take my mind off our separation. Still, I knew that what I was doing was very necessary for me. I was sure it would pay off in the future as I gained some experience in how to handle myself in daily life. Dick wanted to be the one who would bring about whatever maturity I needed to gain. He feared that he would lose me. He loved me so he had to let me go. Only time would tell if we had made the right decisions.

Epilogue

As I soared off to a new life on a new continent with new people destined to be part of this new adventure, I decided to evaluate just what my attitude was in regard to the future. What were my values, my goals, and my viewpoint on life? I settled back to ponder these questions.

Recently, I came across a poem by an unknown author that sums up in a fitting way what my philosophy of life was at that time and still is to this day. I have taken the liberty of modifying some of the lines to match more closely my continuing frame of mind.

The Train of Life

Are you going to ride the train of life looking out toward the rear?
Will you watch the miles of life roll by and mark each passing year?
Will you sit in sad remembrance of the many days gone by?
Will you curse your life for what it was and hang your head and cry?

No, I will not concern myself with that as I take a different vent.
I will look forward to what life holds now and not to what I've spent.
Lord, strap me to your engine as securely as can be.
I want to be out on the front to see what you want me to see.

I want to feel the winds of change as they brush across my face.
I want to see what life unfolds with the help of your loving grace.
I want to see what's coming up, not looking at the past.
Life's too short for yesterdays. It moves along too fast.

So if my road gets bumpy, while I am looking back.
I'll go up front, as I have found my life has jumped the track.
It's all right to remember, as I have my history,
But up front's where it's happening, there is still much mystery.

The enjoyment of living is not where we have been,
It's looking ever forward, to another year and ten.
It's searching all the byways. Never shall I refrain.
For I want to live God's life, so I'm strapped to his own train!

Yahoo! Let's Go!

LaVergne, TN USA
07 April 2010
178380LV00002B/252/A